SAVOR

SAVOR

RUSTIC RECIPES INSPIRED BY
FOREST, FIELD, AND FARM

ILONA OPPENHEIM

ARTISAN

NEW YORK

Library of Congress Cataloging-in-Publication Data

Oppenheim, Ilona, author.
  Savor / Ilona Oppenheim.
      pages cm
  Includes bibliographical references and index.
  ISBN 978-1-57965-666-9
1. Cooking (Natural foods) 2. Outdoor cooking. 3. Wild foods. 4. Oppenheim, Ilona—
Travel. I. Title.
  TX741.O67 2016
  641.3'02—dc23   2015034239

Design by Ilona Oppenheim, produced in collaboration with Gordon de Vries Studio

Artisan books are available at special discounts when purchased in bulk for premiums and sales promotions as well as for fund-raising or educational use. Special editions or book excerpts also can be created to specification. For details, contact the Special Sales Director at the address below, or send an e-mail to specialmarkets@workman.com.

Published by Artisan
A division of Workman Publishing Company, Inc.
225 Varick Street
New York, NY 10014-4381
artisanbooks.com

Published simultaneously in Canada by Thomas Allen & Son, Limited

Printed in China

First printing, February 2016

10 9 8 7 6 5 4 3 2 1

To my husband, Chad, and my kids,

Hendrix and Liloo:

you mean everything to me.

CONTENTS

INTRODUCTION 8

AROUND THE PASTURE 14

FROM THE EARTH 58

INTO THE WILD 122

BY THE FIRE 168

THROUGH THE MILL 212

RESOURCES 264

ACKNOWLEDGMENTS 265

INDEX 266

INTRODUCTION

My house was on the side of a hill, immediately on the edge of the larger wood, in the midst of a young forest of pitch pines and hickories . . .

—HENRY DAVID THOREAU, *WALDEN*

I live in Aspen—not the stereotypical Aspen of glamour and luxury, but the Aspen with snowcapped peaks, crisp mountain air, the scent of evergreens, and the wonderful wildlife that calls it home. I was born in Switzerland and grew up in the foothills of the Alps, but when I was a teenager, my father relocated our family to the United States. Fifteen years later, I moved to the Colorado Rockies; after years in the flat landscape of Florida, I longed for a horizon with peaks and valleys dotted with streams and rivers, forests, rock walls, and narrow paths that open up to breathtaking panoramas. The mountains keep secrets; they envelop me, surprise me, and sometimes overpower me with pure, relentless nature.

Nature also nurtures me. Whether I forage for mushrooms and berries, fish for trout, make a fire, or simply go for a long hike, being outdoors brings me peace of mind.

I love the change of seasons: the expectation of spring, the generosity of summer, the melancholy of fall, and the stillness of winter. On a winter hike there are no distractions, no food to forage; everything is covered in pure white snow. Somehow the monochromatic countryside steadies my mind. I turn inward and find quiet in my head instead of the usual jumble of lists and deadlines. When the light fades, and the colors of the setting sun are absorbed and reflected by the white landscape, I feel one with nature. Treks taken during long summer evenings are mesmerizing, as the moon illuminates the land with sharp shadows and outlines and the black sky glistens with stars. The only sound comes from my footsteps and my rapid breath. Whenever I come home from a hike, my mind is clear, I'm hungry, and all I want to do is cook and eat a great meal.

Being connected to nature is good for my soul, but nature also sustains my family, physically, with its bounty. I get fresh eggs and milk, as well as produce like beets, kale, potatoes, peaches, and apples, from farms in the foothills. We fish for trout in the streams, forage for mushrooms and berries, and often camp overnight and cook over an open fire. We even make tea from pine needles and extract nuts from the pinecones that are scattered on the forest floor.

Growing up in Switzerland, I was taught at an early age to truly enjoy food. My father savored all kinds of cuisine, and he exposed me to everything from bratwurst and pretzels sold by the Zurich street vendors to fresh-caught *Egli* (perch) eaten at a small lakeside cafe, an entire wheel of raclette melted over an open fire at a remote mountain chalet, and fresh oysters and sweetbreads in Europe's finest gourmet restaurants.

My mother always had help in the kitchen, and our meals were made from fresh vegetables, meat, and dairy that arrived at our house every day from the local farms. I wasn't really aware of what took place in our kitchen, but I liked to eat and loved certain foods, like boiled artichokes dipped in vinaigrette and my mother's chocolate mousse. My favorite was the cheese course. I would cut pieces of cheese from the assortment on a large tray and stack them on buttered bread. Not only was this delicious, but I also found it interesting how the different cheeses, made from more or less the same ingredients, really evoked their origins and the way they were created.

My passion for cooking was ignited in the sensible Swiss kitchen of my father's spa, the Clinique La Prairie, where guests came from around the world for beauty treatments and the healthy and delicious cuisine for which it was famous. I was nineteen and living in Miami when my father sent me back to Switzerland to steer me away from Chad, my first boyfriend. I didn't exactly throw myself into this summer job. I started in hospitality, meeting and greeting guests at the clinic's reception desk, but since I am naturally shy, this was not my strength. I was moved to the office, where I was responsible for setting up appointments. This was not a great fit either, and when I inadvertently scheduled a member of the Saudi royal family for the wrong treatment, my father decided to bury me in the kitchen, the least glamorous and most out-of-the-way place.

I didn't know anything about cooking, recipes, or even ingredients. On my first day I made the mistake of confusing basil with parsley, and I got a stern lecture on herbs from the renowned Madame Blaze, the ruler of the subterranean kitchen and a pioneer in healthy gourmet cooking. My schooling in other foods soon followed as the chefs hollered at me to fetch them ingredients from the walk-in refrigerator. I loved the energy in that kitchen. It was like an inner sanctum where I could keep to myself, serve the needs of the kitchen staff, and fulfill my father's wish for me to become engaged in his business. Madame Blaze fascinated me as she crafted magical dishes. In her hands, flour became bread, eggs became crème brûlée, and a basket of fresh vegetables became enough ratatouille to feed all the guests.

I may have been more in the way than useful, but in that kitchen something clicked for me. I enjoyed being lost in the moment as I worked—chopping, mixing, or cleaning—and the intensity allowed no time for diversion.

When I returned to Miami in the fall, I resumed my relationship with Chad, and eventually we got married. I also became a freelance graphic designer, and my flexible work schedule allowed me time to focus on my other love: experimenting in the kitchen. I have always been a fan of cheese, so the first meal I cooked for Chad was a cheese soufflé. It was an absolute disaster, and the next day, in search of help, I bought *Simple to Spectacular* by Jean-Georges Vongerichten. Each chapter started with a simple recipe that, through various steps, turned progressively into a more complicated dish. I cooked every single thing in that book, and went on to spend my spare time reading cookbooks and following the most involved of recipes. I cooked as if my relationship depended on it, and every meal was a

new opportunity to express my feelings for Chad. Some meals took an entire day to create, but I loved every moment, from shopping and finding the right ingredients, to coming home and figuring out the recipe, to cooking and finally sitting down to savor every bite. Each challenging recipe and successful meal gave me more confidence, and cooking became a new way to express myself.

When Chad opened his architectural practice, he would bring potential clients home for dinner. Now what I cooked represented both of us. It was no longer an intimate gesture of my love for him, but a way to help him impress his clients. I was still shy, but making food for others finally brought me out of my shell. Cooking became my own personal language with which to connect with people.

In 2008, one of Chad's clients gave us a copy of Michael Pollan's *The Omnivore's Dilemma*. This book changed my life. After reading it, I felt compelled to source the most wholesome foods I could find and cook them for my family. In preparation for motherhood, and while breast-feeding my son, Hendrix, I bought every book I could find on the subject of "real food" and became obsessed with eating properly so that I could pass on the right nutrition to my child. When Hendrix started on solids, I explored how to make him food from whole ingredients, rather than buy prepared, packaged food. During my research, I became inspired by the writings of Sally Fallon in *Nourishing Traditions*, in which she examines heritage-based, preindustrial methods of preparing healthy and hearty foods. This, in turn, led me to buy my most prized piece of kitchen equipment, a grain mill, and make my own cereals. By the time my daughter, Liloo, was born, my grain mill was in full use, and I was milling nearly all the grains we ate. Soon I began to make my own butter, cheese, yogurt, chocolate, and anything else I could produce from scratch. I wanted to be in control of all the ingredients, which I painstakingly sourced from the best purveyors.

Everything came full circle for me when Chad designed and built our country home. I'll never forget the moment I walked down the hidden stone path and into the newly finished house. I was totally overwhelmed. Never had I expected the stunning views that were framed by each window—we were literally suspended in nature with the Ajax, Highland, and Tiehack Mountains in the foreground and the 14,000-foot Pyramid Peak and the Maroon Bells in the background. Perched alongside a mountain stream, the house blended with its surroundings of large glacier-deposited boulders, pines, aspens, cottonwoods, and serviceberries, and was almost invisible from a distance, as it was composed of those very same materials. Inside, it was cozy and intimate, the perfect atmosphere in which to nurture my family.

I didn't realize how transformative it would be to immerse myself in nature. This wasn't just a beautiful place where our family would grow together—it also unexpectedly connected me to my childhood, and to all the things I left behind when I moved to the United States. This house wasn't merely a mountain retreat; it became the homestead that inspired a deeper love of nature, a more intimate sense of family, and a stronger connection to my cooking and ultimately to the food we eat.

Savor is inspired by my life in the mountains and connecting to nature while savoring good food. With two kids and a busy career, I now prefer to cook simply. I believe that the best food is familiar and comforting, and that recipes don't need to be complicated and intimidating to be delicious. Living so close to nature renewed my interest in wholesome, seasonal food, but no matter where you are, you can get the ingredients from your own garden or a farmers market, CSA, or organic market that stocks locally sourced food. You can forage nearly anywhere, and it is amazing what you can find once you know how to look.

The quality of ingredients and their sourcing is an important part of this book, so rather than organizing the chapters traditionally, I grouped them by where to find the ingredients for the recipes, because that's where every meal I make begins.

When you return from a successful fishing or foraging excursion—or even a trip to the farmers market—you often have more ingredients than you know what to do with. Throughout the book, you'll find ways to make an immediate fresh meal with your newly acquired ingredients, and another recipe or two will offer more ideas for using the same ingredients. For example, when I forage for porcini mushrooms, I make bison steak (see page 141), then dry the unused mushrooms (see page 136) to preserve them for another meal because they spoil quickly. I also provide a recipe that uses the dried mushrooms in pasta sauce (see page 135). The same is the case for berries: During berry season, I often have more on hand than we can eat before they spoil. I love preparing Wild Berry Fool (page 156) with some of the fresh berries; then I preserve the rest by making Mountain Berry Marmalade (page 159) and Fruit Rolls (page 162). When I come home with a lot of trout, I make Trout Amandine (page 144) for dinner. Afterward, I cure the remaining fish and preserve the leftovers by making Trout Jerky (page 148).

I am not a trained chef, but simply a mother who loves to cook for family and friends. *Savor* shows an attainable, wholesome lifestyle from my home in the wilds of the Rockies. But no matter where you live, I encourage you to know where your food comes from and connect to your food sources—something that's difficult to do when you buy shrink-wrapped foods at the supermarket. So buy fresh and buy local, and engage everyone in your family in the adventure of cooking and nourishment. Savor life, and connect to the land—wherever you are.

AROUND
THE
PASTURE

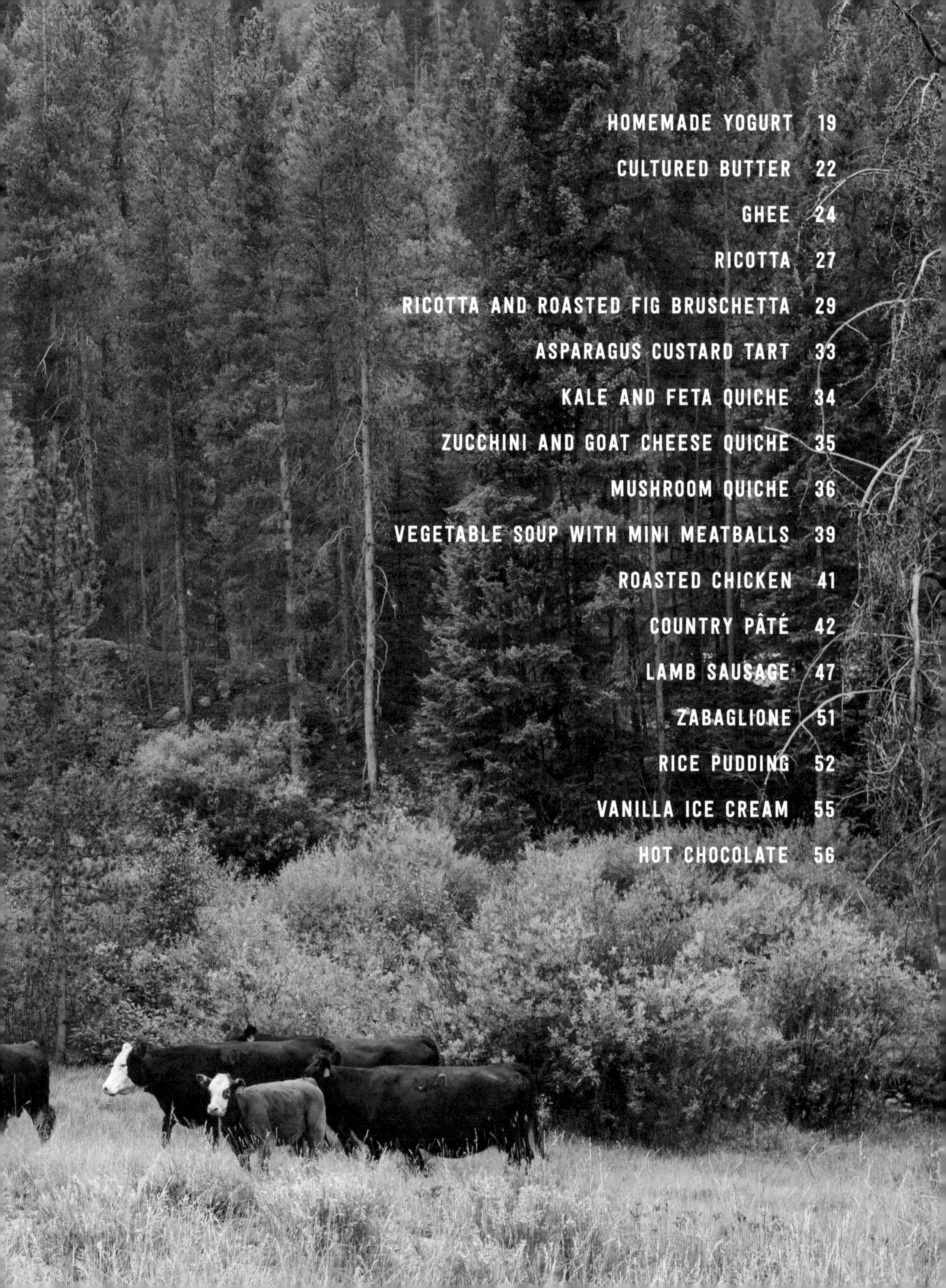

HOMEMADE YOGURT 19

CULTURED BUTTER 22

GHEE 24

RICOTTA 27

RICOTTA AND ROASTED FIG BRUSCHETTA 29

ASPARAGUS CUSTARD TART 33

KALE AND FETA QUICHE 34

ZUCCHINI AND GOAT CHEESE QUICHE 35

MUSHROOM QUICHE 36

VEGETABLE SOUP WITH MINI MEATBALLS 39

ROASTED CHICKEN 41

COUNTRY PÂTÉ 42

LAMB SAUSAGE 47

ZABAGLIONE 51

RICE PUDDING 52

VANILLA ICE CREAM 55

HOT CHOCOLATE 56

When you are faced with food that has been sterilized, fumigated, hydrogenated, hydrolyzed, homogenized, colored, bleached, puffed, exploded, defatted, de-germed, texturized, or if you don't know what has been done to it, the safest rule is not to eat it.

—HELEN AND SCOTT NEARING, *SIMPLE FOOD FOR THE GOOD LIFE*

As a young girl, I walked to my rural Herliberg primary school with my friend Sven. The street on which we both lived turned into a gravel road that led up the hill, and on a clear day we could see the foothills of the Alps and Lake Zürich below. We walked through pastures and orchards and past rushing streams where we'd throw rocks and drop leaves and twigs into the fast-moving water; in the winter, we'd slide and pull each other along the ice and stop to have a snowball fight.

The fertile land that surrounded us was dotted with small family farms where chickens ran freely and snorting piglets pushed from behind a wire fence. As Sven and I walked along, stepping around muddy puddles that gathered in the tire tracks, we'd be greeted by barking dogs, crowing hens, and the sound of cowbells.

Because I grew up among farms, I've always been troubled by the disconnect between mass-produced food and the true sources of our daily nutrition. My children, Hendrix and Liloo, know that food doesn't just appear from an inanimate object like the refrigerator or "grow" at the supermarket. In the mountains, it is easy to connect to the source of our food, and Hendrix and Liloo have visited many farms where we collect warm eggs from the chicken coop and soon after make breakfast at home. We milk the local cows and make yogurt and cream from their fresh, unpasteurized milk.

Whenever I'm in the city, I realize that it's a treasure hunt to find farm-fresh dairy products. But locally grown food is more nutritious and tastes better because it spends less time in transit and is picked when it's ripe.

The recipes in this chapter were inspired by the bounty of pastures where farm animals live in their natural habitat. For instance, farm-fresh eggs, which have intensely orange yolks and are rich in flavor. Generally, they contain more vitamin A, E, and D, more omega-3 fatty acids, more beta-carotene, and less cholesterol and saturated fat than supermarket eggs. In straightforward desserts like Zabaglione (page 51), you'll be able to taste the rich flavor of pasture-raised eggs.

If you have access to grass-fed milk, I encourage you to make your own butter, yogurt, and ricotta cheese as well as ice cream. I use raw milk whenever I can, but in many states, the Food and Drug Administration forbids the sale of raw milk for human consumption and prints warnings that unpasteurized milk can carry dangerous bacteria. So if raw milk is unavailable in your area, or if you choose not to use it, you can make the recipes using nonhomogenized grass-fed milk.

The benefits of grass-fed meat cannot be overestimated. Research has shown that livestock that lives and grazes in pastures produces healthier meat that contains higher levels of omega-3s as well as another good fat called conjugated linoleic acid, or CLA, and is lower in fat and calories.

If you need help finding farms that sell fresh dairy and meat products, go to localharvest.com.

HOMEMADE YOGURT

Making your own yogurt sounds more daunting than it really is, and once you've tasted homemade, you'll never want store-bought again. Most commercial yogurts are full of sugar or other sweeteners and artificial flavoring, whereas homemade yogurt is nothing but milk and culture.

The texture and flavor of homemade yogurt depend on two things: the type of milk and the culture. Avoid ultra-pasteurized milk and try using nonhomogenized milk. Whole milk will give the yogurt a thicker consistency. Using raw whole milk will produce a very creamy yogurt with a smooth taste. Your choice of culture affects the tartness of the yogurt and can create a great range of firmness and texture. To determine which culture you'll like best, read more at Cultures for Health (see Resources, page 264). I like a creamy and mild yogurt, so I use the yogurt starter from Custom Probiotics (see Resources, page 264).

MAKES ABOUT 1 QUART

1 quart whole milk (ideally raw or nonhomogenized grass-fed)
Powdered yogurt starter (amount specified on package) or 3 tablespoons plain yogurt with live cultures

Attach a candy thermometer to a large heavy pot, pour in the milk, and heat it over medium heat to 180°F. Take it off the heat and let cool to 110°F.

Mix in the yogurt starter or plain yogurt. Immediately pour the milk into four 1-cup glass jars with lids, or a 1-liter mason jar.

To incubate, you can use a yogurt maker, which is designed to keep the yogurt at a stable temperature. However, there is really no need to buy this appliance—you can simply let the yogurt incubate in your oven. Keep the oven off and turn on the oven light. Place the closed jars inside and let them incubate for 8 to 9 hours, which makes a creamy yogurt that is not too tart. Refrigerate the yogurt for at least 3 hours before eating. It will keep for 2 weeks in the refrigerator.

This yogurt is great eaten as is, but you can also stir in fruit or flavorings just before serving. If you prefer a thicker, Greek-style yogurt, strain the yogurt through cheesecloth stretched over a bowl. Place the bowl in the refrigerator for 1 hour or overnight—the longer you let it drain, the thicker the yogurt. The whey that drains out can be discarded or saved for another use.

THE BENEFITS OF GRASS-FED MILK

The flavor of unpasteurized farm-fresh milk is superior to that of the regular pasteurized milk you buy at the supermarket. Plus there are health benefits to unpasteurized milk: it includes higher levels of vitamins and minerals, and it is rich in beneficial bacteria and food enzymes, which help the body better digest the milk and absorb the nutrients. There is evidence that raw milk protects against asthma, allergies, and other immune-related diseases. However, if you don't have access to raw, farm-fresh milk from a trusted source, try to find nonhomogenized grass-fed milk at your local health food store. Homogenization is a process by which all the fat molecules in the milk are mechanically forced to be the same size. Nonhomogenized milk has a cream layer on top, which is a natural occurrence, giving the milk a clean, full-bodied flavor.

Also, try to stay away from ultra-pasteurized milk, which is heated to a higher temperature than regular pasteurized milk. This is done to increase the milk's shelf life, but the treatment also changes the milk's taste and texture and damages the vitamins, minerals, and other nutrients. It also kills all the beneficial bacteria in milk that are needed to properly digest and absorb its nutrients. Without these, the body may perceive the proteins in the milk as foreign and mount an immune response, which can lead to lactose intolerance.

CULTURED BUTTER

When I was a child, our butter came from a local farm and was delivered to our house along with milk and other dairy products. The butter was naturally golden in color and had a rich, tangy flavor. In Colorado, I again have access to raw milk and have rediscovered the amazing taste of butter made from farm-fresh cream. If you can't find raw cream, look for nonhomogenized grass-fed cream at your local health food store. Don't make this recipe if all you can find is ultra-pasteurized cream—the result won't be the same.

To get the best flavor and nutritional benefits from your cultured butter, I recommend adding piima (see Resources, page 264). Piima is a culture that helps milk coagulate and turns butter into a beneficial probiotic food. This Scandinavian culture is derived from the milk of cows that feed on the butterwort plant. Butter made with piima culture comes out tangy with a nuance of a mild cheese flavor and a creamy texture. If you plan on making butter regularly, it is worth starting with this culture. Each time you make butter, set aside a small portion of the butter culture and use it to make your next batch.

MAKES 1 CUP

2 cups heavy cream (ideally raw or nonhomogenized grass-fed)

1 tablespoon piima culture (see Note)

To culture the cream, pour the cream and piima culture into a 1-pint glass jar with a lid. Don't tighten the lid completely; you want air to get in. Leave the jar undisturbed at room temperature until the mixture thickens, approximately 24 hours. Refrigerate for at least 5 hours.

Remove 1 tablespoon of the culture, place it in a small covered glass jar, and refrigerate. You'll use this for your next batch of butter.

Use the rest of the thickened cream to make the butter. Close the jar tightly and shake it, or pour the cream into a blender and mix, until the butter begins to clump together and the watery buttermilk separates, about 5 minutes in the blender. Discard the buttermilk or refrigerate it for another use, such as making pancake batter.

Place the butter in a sieve and wash it with cold water. Make sure you wash the butter until the water runs clear or it will become rancid after a few days. Transfer the butter to a container with a lid and refrigerate. It should keep for up to 3 weeks (smell the butter before using it to make sure it has not become rancid).

NOTE

You can make butter without using the piima culture. Skip the culturing process and begin the recipe by pouring the cream into a glass jar or a blender and shaking or blending it, as described above.

VARIATIONS

ROASTED WALNUT BUTTER
Using a wooden spoon, mix 1 cup room-temperature butter with
¼ cup chopped roasted walnut pieces and ¼ teaspoon flaky sea salt.

HONEY BUTTER
Mix 1 cup room-temperature butter with 3 tablespoons honeycomb
in a blender for just a few seconds until well combined.

GHEE

Ghee is a type of clarified butter traditionally used in Indian cooking. Due to its high smoke point, it is great for high-temperature cooking and is a good alternative to vegetable oils. The process of making ghee is similar to that for clarified butter, but the butter is cooked for a longer time alongside the milk solids, which gives it that great nutty taste. Ghee is the butterfat that is left over after the water and milk solids are removed from the butter.

MAKES ABOUT 1¾ CUPS

1 pound (4 sticks) high-quality unsalted butter

Cut the butter into squares and place in a medium saucepan. Bring to a boil over medium heat, then reduce the heat to medium-low and simmer the butter. After about 8 minutes, when the foam subsides and the butter turns a golden color, start stirring as it continues to simmer. When the butter foams a second time, after another 8 minutes, turn off the heat.

Let the butter cool down for a couple of minutes. Line a sieve with cheesecloth and set it over a bowl. Strain the butter through the cheesecloth. Discard the milk solids that remain in the cheesecloth.

Store the ghee in an airtight container at room temperature for up to 3 months. (Removing the milk solids inhibits spoilage, so it is okay to store at room temperature.) If you store it in the refrigerator, you can keep it for up to 1 year.

RICOTTA

You'll be surprised at how easy it is to make ricotta cheese at home: just heat milk to the boiling point, lower the heat, and stir in vinegar. The curds that begin to form are ricotta. It's delicious while it is still warm; spread fresh ricotta on toast and top with honey, olive oil, or aged balsamic vinegar. It's also great on pizza with a drizzle of truffle oil and a sprinkle of coarse salt.

MAKES ABOUT 1 CUP

3 cups whole milk (ideally raw or nonhomogenized grass-fed)
1 cup half-and-half (ideally raw or nonhomogenized grass-fed)
1 teaspoon fine sea salt
3 tablespoons white wine vinegar

Bring the milk, half-and-half, and salt to a boil in a heavy pot over medium-high heat. Stir occasionally to prevent scorching. As soon as the mixture starts to boil, reduce the heat to low and add the vinegar. Simmer while stirring very gently until the mixture curdles, 1 to 2 minutes.

Line a large sieve with several layers of fine-mesh cheesecloth and place it over a large bowl. Pour the mixture into the sieve and let it drain at room temperature for 1 hour. Discard the drained liquid or save it for other uses, such as soaking your grains.

Enjoy the ricotta right away while it's still warm, or refrigerate in an airtight container for up to 4 days.

RICOTTA AND ROASTED FIG BRUSCHETTA

Figs are one of the oldest cultivated fruit crops in the world and a great source of fiber and potassium. They appear at my local farmers market in late August, but since the mountain climate is too harsh for fig trees, the farmers bring them up from the valley. Figs have two seasons: a short early-summer season and late summer, when the main crop comes in. The figs in this recipe are roasted with fresh orange juice to bring out a caramelized texture and flavor and used as a topping with homemade ricotta on toasted Hearty Bread.

SERVES 4

8 fresh figs, cut in half

Juice of 1 orange

4 slices Hearty Bread (page 243), or other rustic whole-grain bread

¾ cup ricotta cheese (see page 27)

4 teaspoons extra-virgin olive oil

Pinch of flaky sea salt

Preheat the oven to 400°F.

Place the figs on a rimmed baking sheet. Pour the orange juice over them and toss them in the juice. Turn the figs cut side up and roast until soft and caramelized, about 10 minutes.

While the figs are roasting, toast the bread in the hot oven until just colored.

Spread the ricotta on the toast and top with the roasted figs. Drizzle with olive oil and sprinkle with salt.

ASPARAGUS CUSTARD TART

This custard recipe is a great basis for experimenting with different fillings—you can also vary just the cheese to alter the flavor. You can omit the asparagus and use an additional three leeks or try experimenting with other vegetables. To eliminate extra moisture, it is best to precook the vegetables before adding them to the tart. And a soggy crust can ruin a tart, so take the extra step of baking the crust before filling it.

SERVES 4

Butter, for coating the tart pan
Savory Tart Dough (page 247)
1 pound asparagus, trimmed
1 teaspoon ghee (see page 24)
1 leek, white and light green parts only, finely chopped
1 cup half-and-half (ideally raw or nonhomogenized grass-fed)
3 large pasture-raised eggs
¾ teaspoon fine sea salt
½ teaspoon freshly ground black pepper
⅓ cup freshly grated Parmesan cheese
1 tablespoon chopped fresh rosemary

Preheat the oven to 350°F.

Butter an 11-inch tart pan. Gently press the tart dough into the bottom of the pan and up the sides. Bake the crust for 10 minutes.

In a large bowl, set up an ice bath. Fill a medium pot halfway with water and bring to a boil. Add the asparagus and cook until crisp-tender, about 3 minutes. Drain the asparagus and submerge in the ice bath. After it has cooled, drain again.

Melt the ghee in a small sauté pan and sauté the leek until very tender, about 10 minutes. Remove from the heat.

Whisk together the half-and-half, eggs, salt, and pepper in a medium bowl. Add the leek, Parmesan, and rosemary.

Arrange the asparagus like spokes in a wheel in the prebaked tart shell. Pour the custard over the asparagus.

Bake until the top browns and a knife inserted near the center comes out clean, about 30 minutes. Serve warm or at room temperature. Leftovers will keep for up to 2 days covered in the refrigerator; bring to room temperature or reheat in the oven before serving.

KALE AND FETA QUICHE

A quiche is an easy meal that works well for breakfast, a light lunch, or a quick dinner when served with a side of salad. Quiche is easy to customize, too. You'll find two other options following this recipe, but you can use any combination of ingredients—leftover cooked vegetables or meat and cheese—to make your own creation. Leftover quiche can be kept in the refrigerator, but it's tastier at room temperature; I often serve it as picnic food.

SERVES 2

Butter, for coating the ramekins

1 teaspoon ghee (see page 24)

1 tablespoon finely chopped leek

2/3 cup coarsely torn kale leaves

2 large pasture-raised eggs

2 tablespoons feta cheese

Pinch of fine sea salt

Freshly ground black pepper

Preheat the oven to 375°F. Coat two 5-inch ramekins with butter.

Heat the ghee in a large skillet over medium heat. Add the leek and sauté until tender, about 8 minutes. Add the kale and sauté until wilted, about 2 minutes more. Let cool.

In a small bowl, mix together the eggs and feta and season with salt and pepper. Add the kale mixture.

Divide the mixture between the ramekins. Bake until a knife inserted near the center comes out clean, 20 to 30 minutes. Serve warm or at room temperature.

ZUCCHINI AND GOAT CHEESE QUICHE

I am never without zucchini when the summer season is in full swing. This recipe is an easy way to make good use of the abundance. Since zucchini has a very high water content, it is important to drain it well so the quiche does not end up soggy. The goat cheese adds a great creamy texture and tangy flavor to the dish.

SERVES 2

Butter, for coating the ramekins

½ zucchini, thinly sliced (about ½ cup)

Fine sea salt

1 teaspoon ghee (see page 24)

¼ onion, chopped

¼ teaspoon fresh thyme

2 large pasture-raised eggs

2 tablespoons goat cheese

1 tablespoon freshly grated Parmesan cheese

Freshly ground black pepper

Preheat the oven to 375°F. Coat two 5-inch ramekins with butter.

Place the zucchini in a strainer and sprinkle evenly with ¾ teaspoon salt. Let drain for 30 minutes, then spread out on paper towels to drain for another 30 minutes.

Heat ½ teaspoon of the ghee in a small skillet over medium heat. Add the onion and sauté until soft, about 10 minutes. Set aside. Heat the remaining ½ teaspoon ghee in a medium skillet over medium heat. Add the zucchini and thyme and sauté over medium heat until tender, about 5 minutes. Let cool.

In a small bowl, mix together the eggs, goat cheese, and Parmesan, and season with salt and pepper to taste. Add the zucchini and onion.

Divide the mixture between the prepared ramekins. Bake until a knife inserted near the center comes out clean, 20 to 30 minutes. Serve warm or at room temperature.

MUSHROOM QUICHE

Baking quiche in individual ramekins makes for easy serving; they can be eaten right out of the dish they're cooked in. If chanterelle mushrooms are not in season, you can substitute other wild mushrooms or shiitake mushrooms, although the flavor will be different.

SERVES 2

Butter, for coating the ramekins

2 teaspoons ghee (see page 24)

½ cup chanterelle mushrooms, roughly chopped

2 tablespoons finely chopped shallots

1 garlic clove, crushed

¼ teaspoon fresh thyme leaves

Fine sea salt and freshly ground black pepper

2 large pasture-raised eggs

1 tablespoon half-and-half (ideally raw or nonhomogenized grass-fed)

Preheat the oven to 375°F. Coat two 5-inch ramekins with butter.

Heat the ghee in a large skillet over medium heat. Add the mushrooms. Stirring often, let them sear until browned, about 10 minutes. Add the shallots, garlic, and thyme and sauté until the liquid from the mushrooms has evaporated, about 5 more minutes. The edges should be crispy and the texture firm. Season with salt and pepper to taste. Let cool.

In a small bowl, mix together the eggs and half-and-half and season with salt and pepper. Add the mushroom mixture.

Divide the mixture between the prepared ramekins. Bake until a knife inserted near the center comes out clean, 20 to 30 minutes. Serve warm or at room temperature.

VEGETABLE SOUP WITH MINI MEATBALLS

Vegetable soup is a great way to combine a variety of your garden's vegetables into one healthy dish. The broth is light and flavorful; adding meatballs makes it a heartier meal.

SERVES 6

1 pound freshly ground grass-fed beef (20% fat is best)

1 garlic clove, smashed and finely chopped

1½ teaspoons fine sea salt

1 teaspoon freshly ground pepper

2 tablespoons ghee (see page 24)

1 leek, white and light green parts only, chopped

2 shallots, chopped

2 large tomatoes, chopped

2 quarts chicken stock, preferably homemade

4 carrots, chopped

2 celery stalks, chopped

2 medium potatoes, chopped

1 branch of fresh thyme

1 whole bunch of fresh cilantro

Chopped fresh flat-leaf parsley, for serving

Chopped scallions, white parts only, for serving

Combine the ground beef, garlic, salt, and pepper in a medium bowl. Use your hands to form the meat into ¾-inch balls. Set aside on a platter.

In a stockpot, melt 1 tablespoon of the ghee over medium-low heat. Add the meatballs and sauté them until the underside has browned, about 2 minutes. Turn the meatballs and brown on all sides until cooked through, about 2 minutes longer. Transfer the meatballs to a plate.

Add the remaining tablespoon ghee to the same pot and sauté the leek over medium-high heat until soft, about 2 minutes. Add the shallots and sauté until browned, about 7 minutes. Add the tomatoes and sauté for another 5 minutes. Add the meatballs to the vegetable mixture.

Add the chicken stock, carrots, celery, potatoes, and thyme to the pot. Cover, let come to a boil, then lower the heat and simmer for 1 hour. Add the cilantro and cook for another 5 minutes. Remove the cilantro and thyme branch. Garnish with chopped parsley and scallions. Leftovers will keep for 3 days in the refrigerator.

ROASTED CHICKEN

The freshest chickens come straight from the farm, but you can also get a pastured chicken at better supermarkets. This roasted chicken can be served directly from the pan, where it's cooked with lots of lemon, garlic, and shallots. Spoon the caramelized shallots and sweet roasted garlic over the top and serve with Crispy Roasted Potatoes (page 95) on the side.

SERVES 6

One 4-pound pasture-raised whole chicken

3 fresh rosemary sprigs, finely chopped

6 fresh thyme sprigs, finely chopped

6 fresh parsley sprigs, finely chopped

3 tablespoons unsalted butter, at room temperature

Fine sea salt and freshly ground black pepper

2 heads of garlic, tops cut off, plus 3 garlic cloves, finely chopped

4 lemons, cut in half

3 tablespoons ghee (see page 24)

8 shallots, peeled and cut in half

Preheat the oven to 400°F.

Remove the giblets from the cavity of the chicken; discard or save them to make broth or gravy. Rinse the chicken inside and out and dry with paper towels. Tuck the wings under the bird and truss the legs to keep them from drying out.

In a small bowl, use a fork to mash together half the rosemary, thyme, and parsley with the butter and season with ¼ teaspoon salt and ⅛ teaspoon pepper. Starting at the neck cavity, gently loosen the skin from the breasts and drumsticks; slide the butter mixture under the skin.

Combine the 3 finely chopped garlic cloves and the juice from 2 of the lemon halves in a small bowl. Rub the mixture inside the cavity and on the outside of the chicken. Stuff the remaining herbs into the cavity and season the chicken with ½ teaspoon salt and ¼ teaspoon pepper.

On the stove over low heat, melt 2 tablespoons of the ghee in an extra-large ovenproof roasting pan. Add the shallots, cut side down, cover, and fry for 3 minutes. Add the remaining lemon halves and the garlic heads, cut side down, cover the pan, and fry for another 5 minutes. Remove the vegetables and lemons and set aside.

Raise the heat to medium-high and add the remaining tablespoon ghee to the pan. Add the chicken, breast side up, and brown it, about 2 minutes. Turn it over and brown it for another 2 minutes. Return the vegetables and lemons to the pan. Place the pan in the oven.

Bake for 30 minutes. Flip the chicken so the breast is up. Cook until the juice runs clear, about another 40 minutes. Let the chicken rest at room temperature for 10 minutes before carving. Transfer the chicken to a large platter. Squeeze the lemon halves over the chicken and spoon the garlic and shallots around the chicken before serving.

COUNTRY PÂTÉ

Making your own pâté is easier than you might think. You can use your own meat grinder to grind the pork, chicken breast, and liver or buy preground meat and chop the liver. Be sure to use organic, grass-fed meat. I make this pâté in a traditional earthenware dish, but you can use any ovenproof dish. If your dish does not have a lid, simply cover it with foil.

SERVES 15

1 tablespoon ghee (see page 24)

1 small yellow onion, chopped

1 garlic clove, chopped

1 pound pork, freshly ground

1 pound chicken breast, freshly ground

8 ounces pork or beef liver, chopped into ½-inch pieces

⅓ cup freshly ground stale bread

⅓ cup heavy cream (ideally raw or nonhomogenized grass-fed)

¼ cup cognac

1 large pasture-raised egg

2 tablespoons coarsely chopped fresh flat-leaf parsley

1 tablespoon fine sea salt

½ teaspoon ground allspice

½ teaspoon mace

1 teaspoon fresh thyme leaves

¼ teaspoon freshly ground black pepper

½ cup pistachios

16 slices of thick-cut bacon (1 pound)

Crusty bread and butter, for serving

SPECIAL EQUIPMENT
Two 3-by-10-inch earthenware terrines

continued

COUNTRY PÂTÉ *continued*

Preheat the oven to 350°F.

Melt the ghee in a small sauté pan over medium-low heat. Add the onion and garlic and sauté, stirring frequently, until soft, about 10 minutes.

Combine the ground pork and chicken in a large bowl. Add the chopped liver and combine well with the ground meats.

Add the bread crumbs, cream, cognac, egg, parsley, salt, allspice, mace, thyme, pepper, and pistachios. Stir until well combined.

Line the terrines with the bacon slices, arranging 8 slices across the width of each terrine. Fill with the pâté mixture. Fold the bacon slices over, covering the pâté. Cover each terrine with a lid or with aluminum foil.

Bake until the center of the terrine reaches 150°F on an instant-read thermometer, about 1 hour 40 minutes. Let cool for 2 hours, cover with a lid or wrap in parchment paper, and refrigerate for about 1 day to allow the flavors to develop. Serve the pâté at room temperature with crusty bread and butter. It will keep for 1 week in the refrigerator in an airtight container.

LAMB SAUSAGE

When making lamb sausages, you don't need to waste money on expensive cuts of meat. Instead, try using organic cuts from the shoulder, neck, or breast, preferably bought from a local farm or butcher. If you don't have a meat grinder, you can pulse the meat in batches in a food processor. When grinding the meat, it's important that both the meat and the food processor blade are very cold so the meat does not turn into mush (put the food processor blade in the freezer for 30 minutes before using). You can also ask the butcher to grind your meat for you.

You'll find a wide selection of sausage stuffers and meat grinders in every price range online or in kitchen supply stores (see Resources, page 264). If you own a stand mixer, you can get a food grinder attachment and a sausage stuffer kit. It's an economical solution and doesn't take up much storage space. If you don't have a sausage stuffer, shape the sausage meat into patties and fry them in a pan.

MAKES TEN TO TWELVE 6-INCH SAUSAGE LINKS

Natural hog casings (optional; see Resources, page 264)

2 pounds lamb shoulder, neck, or breast

½ pound pork butt

¼ cup finely chopped shallots

1½ teaspoons extra-virgin olive oil

2 tablespoons Harissa (recipe follows)

1 tablespoon finely chopped fresh flat-leaf parsley

1 teaspoon fine sea salt, or more to taste

Ghee (see page 24), if frying the sausage in a pan

Mustard and fresh bread, for serving

SPECIAL EQUIPMENT
Meat grinder
Sausage stuffer

Soak the hog casings, if using, for 1 hour in a bowl filled with tepid water. Rinse well with cool water. Place the casings in a sieve to drain.

Cut the lamb and pork butt into 1-inch pieces. Chill the meat and the grinder or blade in the freezer for 30 minutes. Using the finest grind on your machine, grind the meat mixture into a large bowl.

Add the shallots, olive oil, harissa, parsley, and salt to the bowl with the meat. Mix by hand or with a stand mixer using the paddle attachment until the meat binds together and the mixture is very sticky.

You can test the flavor by frying a small patty in a sauté pan. Taste and adjust the seasoning if needed.

continued

To form the sausage into links, thread a hog casing over the sausage stuffer. Tie a knot at the end of the casing. Hold the casing as you feed the meat through the grinder. At every 6 inches, pinch and twist the sausages into links in opposite directions. Once you have stuffed the casing with the sausage, tie a knot at the other end. Refrigerate the sausages and repeat with the remaining filling and casings. You can keep the sausages in the refrigerator for up to 3 days.

If not using casings, form the meat mixture into patties. Heat a skillet over medium-low heat. Coat with ghee and sauté the patties until brown on both sides and cooked through, about 5 minutes per side.

To cook the links, grill over indirect heat, turning frequently, or heat a skillet over medium-low heat, coat with ghee, and sauté until cooked through, 10 to 15 minutes. Serve with mustard and freshly baked Hearty Bread (page 243) or other rustic whole-grain bread.

HARISSA

Harissa is a hot chile pepper paste from Tunisia. The main ingredients—roasted red peppers, various hot chile peppers, garlic, coriander, caraway, and cumin seeds—make for a spicy and strong condiment that you can use to jazz up snacks, appetizers, and many other dishes.

MAKES ABOUT ⅔ CUP

2 dried or 3 fresh chiles of your choice (optional)

1 red bell pepper, roasted, seeds removed

1 teaspoon caraway seeds

1 teaspoon coriander seeds

½ teaspoon cumin seeds

3 garlic cloves

1 teaspoon fine sea salt

1 teaspoon lemon juice

1 tablespoon extra-virgin olive oil, plus more
for sealing the surface

If using dried chiles, place them in a heatproof bowl and cover with boiling water. Let sit for 30 minutes, until softened. Drain.

Cut the tops off the dried or fresh chiles and remove the seeds. Put the chiles in a mini food processor along with the roasted red pepper, caraway seeds, coriander seeds, cumin seeds, garlic, salt, and lemon juice. Purée while slowly pouring in the olive oil until a smooth paste forms.

If not using immediately, transfer to an airtight container and cover the surface of the harissa with a layer of olive oil. It will keep for a month in the refrigerator.

ZABAGLIONE

Zabaglione is a luscious custard dessert with Italian origins. The best zabaglione is made with farm-fresh eggs, which create a richer, more buttery custard than store-bought eggs. I also use a high-quality Marsala wine, but you can use Madeira, Moscato d'Asti, or vin santo. Serve this creamy dessert warm, poured over berries with a side of biscotti.

SERVES 4 TO 6

4 large pasture-raised egg yolks, at room temperature

2 tablespoons organic cane sugar

¼ cup Marsala wine

1 vanilla bean (optional)

Fresh berries, for serving

Biscotti (page 261), for serving (optional)

Combine the egg yolks and sugar in a large stainless steel bowl and whisk until pale yellow and creamy. Slowly whisk in the wine. Split the vanilla bean, if using, in half lengthwise and scrape the seeds into the egg yolk mixture. Discard the bean.

Fill a small saucepan (the diameter should be slightly less than that of the bowl) with 1 inch of water and bring to a simmer. Prepare a bain-marie by placing the mixing bowl over the saucepan; it should not touch the water. Using a wire whisk or an electric hand mixer, beat the mixture until frothy and tripled in volume. Make sure the water does not get too hot or the eggs will scramble. The custard should be ready in 8 to 10 minutes, when it is transformed into a pale, foamy light sauce.

Serve immediately. Put berries in individual serving bowls and pour the warm custard over them. Serve with biscotti on the side, if desired.

RICE PUDDING

For many of us, rice pudding evokes comfort as well as indulgence. This version is creamy and nostalgic and takes very little work. Traditionally, rice pudding is made on the stovetop and requires constant stirring, but if you prepare it in a slow cooker you can leave it unattended. It cooks for 4 hours and will fill your kitchen with the wonderful smells of cinnamon and spice.

SERVES 4

½ cup short-grain brown rice

3 cups whole milk (ideally raw or nonhomogenized grass-fed)

2 tablespoons raw honey

1 cinnamon stick

¼ teaspoon fine sea salt

Pinch of nutmeg

1 large pasture-raised egg yolk, lightly beaten

⅓ cup raisins

SPECIAL EQUIPMENT
Slow cooker

Place the rice in a medium bowl, pour in enough water to cover, and soak overnight at room temperature.

In the morning, drain the rice and put in the slow cooker along with the milk, honey, cinnamon stick, salt, and nutmeg.

Cover and bring to a boil on high heat, then reduce the heat to low. Simmer for 2 hours. Stir, then simmer for another 2 hours.

Temper the egg yolk by stirring a small amount of the hot mixture into it to gently warm the yolk without cooking it. Pour the yolk into the cooker. Mix in the raisins. Cook uncovered, stirring, until thickened, about 5 minutes. Turn off the cooker and let the pudding cool to the desired temperature.

Serve warm or at room temperature. You can refrigerate leftovers for up to 3 days.

VANILLA ICE CREAM

I always look for ways to avoid using refined sugar, so this recipe incorporates maple syrup instead. The result is an amazingly rich and creamy ice cream that has the perfect amount of sweetness. It takes only four ingredients, but you *will* need an ice cream maker.

SERVES 6 TO 8

3¾ cups half-and-half (ideally raw or nonhomogenized grass-fed)
2 vanilla beans
10 large pasture-raised egg yolks
⅓ cup maple syrup, raw honey, or date syrup

SPECIAL EQUIPMENT
Ice cream maker

Pour the half-and-half into a medium heavy-bottomed pot. Split the vanilla beans in half lengthwise and scrape the seeds into the half-and-half. Put the scraped-out beans in the pot, too. Bring to a boil over medium-high heat, stirring occasionally.

Meanwhile, in a large bowl, beat the egg yolks and your sweetener of choice with a whisk until well combined.

Once the half-and-half comes to a boil, reduce the temperature to low. Gradually whisk about 1 cup of the hot liquid into the yolk mixture to temper the eggs. Add the yolk mixture to the remaining half-and-half in the pot, whisking constantly until the mixture thickens slightly, about 1 minute.

Remove the vanilla bean. Let the liquid cool down before pouring it into the ice cream maker. Churn the mixture until it reaches the desired consistency (follow your ice cream maker's instructions). For a creamy gelato-style ice cream, churning takes about 35 minutes. Serve right away, or for a thicker consistency, place it in the freezer for an hour before eating.

HOT CHOCOLATE

After a day outdoors playing in the snow, there is nothing better than a cup of cocoa to warm you from the inside. For an extra-special treat, top the hot chocolate with freshly whipped cream and chocolate shavings. This recipe uses high-quality dark chocolate, which gives the cocoa an intense flavor. For a sweeter drink, increase the sugar to your liking, or use chocolate with a lower percentage of cacao.

SERVES 4

1 quart whole milk (ideally raw or nonhomogenized grass-fed)

1 tablespoon organic cane sugar, plus 1 tablespoon for whipping cream, if using

1 cinnamon stick

Pinch of fine sea salt

8 ounces dark chocolate, at least 70% cacao, chopped into small pieces

1 cup whipping cream (ideally raw or nonhomogenized grass-fed; optional)

½ teaspoon vanilla extract (if making whipped cream)

Pinch of ground cinnamon (optional)

Chocolate shavings or cocoa powder (optional)

Heat the milk, 1 tablespoon sugar, the cinnamon stick, and salt in a medium saucepan over medium-high heat. Stir occasionally. When the milk begins to simmer, lower the heat and stir in the chocolate. Whisk until smooth.

Cook at a low simmer until the chocolate mixture thickens, about 5 minutes. Remove and discard the cinnamon stick.

If making whipped cream: Pour the whipping cream, 1 tablespoon sugar, and vanilla into a large bowl and beat by hand with a whisk or an electric mixer until soft peaks form.

Pour the hot chocolate into mugs and, if desired, top with a dollop of whipped cream and a sprinkling of cinnamon, chocolate shavings, or cocoa powder.

FROM THE
EARTH

ROOT VEGETABLE CHIPS 65

BAKED POTATO CHIPS 68

KALE SALAD 70

BEET SALAD 76

TWENTY-FOUR-HOUR ONION SOUP 80

BOILED ARTICHOKES 82

GARLIC SCAPE COMPOUND BUTTER 85

ZUCCHINI TART 86

TOMATO TART 91

SUN-DRIED TOMATOES 92

CRISPY ROASTED POTATOES 95

RÖSTI 96

STEWED PEARS 98

PEAR CRISP 100

SLOW-COOKED APPLESAUCE 105

MULLED APPLE CIDER 107

PEACH MARMALADE 108

PEACH TART 113

PLUM COBBLER 117

CLAFOUTIS 120

The soil is the great connector of lives, the source and destination of all. It is the healer and restorer and resurrector, by which disease passes into health, age into youth, death into life.

—WENDELL BERRY, *THE UNSETTLING OF AMERICA: CULTURE AND AGRICULTURE*

When my husband, Chad, and I traveled to the Lattari Mountains in Italy, I experienced the difference between American and Italian produce for the first time. The tomatoes, fennel, olive oil, bread, and almost everything else on the Amalfi Coast is served simply, without lots of added spices or complicated dressings, and tastes delicious nevertheless. Eggplants, zucchini, and peaches look pretty much the same but taste completely different in the United States. Eating in Italy made me question all my fancy recipes, sauces, and ingredients and wonder whether the inherent flavor of our so-called fresh food had been lost in mass production. I felt frustrated and even a bit hopeless, but I was also inspired.

Not long after our trip to Italy, Chad worked on a project with Eli Zabar, the visionary New York City restaurateur. We were invited to spend a few days at the Zabar family home in the South of France. While Chad and Eli worked, I sat at the old kitchen table, which was piled with baskets of tomatoes from Eli's garden, and studied his entire culinary library. When Eli realized that I was interested in cooking, he took me under his wing, and we visited several of the farmers markets that Provence is known for. It was the middle of summer and the range of fresh produce was exhilarating. While he rubbed rosemary twigs between his fingers and held them up to my nose, Eli told me that cooking is all about keeping it simple and letting the natural, fresh ingredients shine. This was a new approach for me. I'd spent years following complicated recipes; now here was a culinary genius telling me that fresh ingredients would do their own work and that what we cook ought to be dictated by what is available: the gifts from the earth that day, that week, that summer. Together we selected the prime, sun-ripened figs, plums, and berries harvested that morning and prepared salads with French greens I didn't even recognize. Once I was back in America, I made it my priority to find only fresh ingredients and use the natural flavor of what was in season, grown locally and organically.

In Colorado, I can count on Jack Reed to provide me with locally grown seasonal fruit and vegetables. His eclectic Roots and Shoots farm stand is a favorite on the local food scene, and the fact that he's not always so easy to track down makes him even more popular. He stocks his fifty-square-foot space with produce that he gathers from many different local farms and keeps the recent harvest—everything from peaches, beets, and cucumbers to broccoli rabe and fresh garlic shoots—in a beat-up pickup truck that's parked in a nearby alley. Then he constantly runs back and forth to restock his makeshift table.

I stop the car at every farm stand I pass; I never know what I will find, but I do know it'll be a fresh, seasonal harvest that will inspire our next meal. Whenever possible, I take my children, Hendrix and Liloo, to pick our own fruit and vegetables at T.R.E.E. (Together Regenerating the Environment through Education), an educational farm that was started to address the disconnect between society and its food sources. There is nothing better than seeing kids connect to the origins of their food by taking peas right off the stalk or digging for carrots and washing and eating them right then and there.

I'm a member of a local CSA, and when I receive my weekly share from Sustainable Settings, a great organic farm and learning center at the base of Mount Sopris, I celebrate with a big feast to enjoy the fruits and vegetables at their peak.

Local CSAs offer fresh, seasonal produce, but you'll find that more and more CSAs have started to diversify with a larger range of foods, including natural dairy products, grass-fed meat, even fresh flour and, depending on the location, seafood.

This chapter celebrates the earth's bounty throughout the seasons with recipes for dishes that can be eaten anytime, like Slow-Cooked Applesauce (page 105) and Peach Marmalade (page 108) that you can make in batches large or small. Root Vegetable Chips (page 65), Kale Salad (page 70), and Twenty-Four-Hour Onion Soup (page 80) are all recipes that work throughout the year and make use of hardy vegetables. Of course, summer is the most exciting time for cooking with food that has come straight from the earth, and the innate flavor of freshly picked fruit and vegetables makes simple recipes like Plum Cobbler (page 117), Garlic Scape Compound Butter (page 85), and vegetable tarts (see pages 86 and 91) an instant success.

To find out where, when, and how you can be part of a CSA, see Resources (page 264).

ROOT VEGETABLE CHIPS

If you leave the peel on the vegetables, these potato chip substitutes will retain the extra nutritional benefits found in the veggie skins. These chips are best served on the day they're made, but they will stay fresh for about three days in an airtight container. Give them to your kids for an after-school treat, but grown-ups will be tempted to snack on them, too.

SERVES 4

2 medium beets, scrubbed and tops removed
1 sweet potato, scrubbed
1 tablespoon extra-virgin olive oil
1 teaspoon flaky sea salt

Preheat the oven to 250°F. Line two large baking sheets with parchment paper.

Slice the vegetables about ⅛ inch thick. Use a mandoline, if you have one, to create even pieces. Place the beet slices in one bowl and the sweet potatoes in another.

Divide the olive oil and salt between the bowls and toss the slices to coat. Place on the prepared baking sheets without letting the slices touch.

Place the baking sheets in the oven. Rotate the pans after 1 hour and continue to bake until crisp, a total of 1 hour 50 minutes to 2 hours for the beets and 1 hour 40 minutes for the sweet potatoes. Transfer the chips to a large bowl and serve immediately. Leftovers will keep for up to 3 days in an airtight container.

BAKED POTATO CHIPS

Potato chips often get a bad rep because they are filled with additives and fats, and they lose their nutritional value while being processed. But when potatoes come straight from the ground, they are a great source of potassium, magnesium, and vitamin C. With these homemade baked chips, you can retain the nutritious benefits of the potatoes without any of the unhealthy side effects and make everyone happy to eat them, too.

SERVES 4

2 medium russet potatoes

2 tablespoons chopped fresh rosemary

2 teaspoons extra-virgin olive oil

1 teaspoon flaky sea salt

Preheat the oven to 350°F. Line a baking sheet with parchment paper.

Thinly slice the potatoes as evenly as possible; use a mandoline if you have one. Wash the potato slices under cold water and dry them with paper towels (see Note).

In a medium bowl, combine the potato slices with the rosemary, olive oil, and salt. Place them on the prepared baking sheet in one layer.

Bake until the potatoes are crisp and golden, about 30 minutes, depending on the thickness. Transfer the chips that are ready to a serving bowl, and bake the ones that are not yet crisp for another couple of minutes. Although the chips are best served fresh, leftovers can be stored in an airtight container for 1 to 2 weeks.

NOTE

Washing the potato slices will get rid of the starch and make the chips crisper.

KALE SALAD

Kale was first cultivated in about 2000 BC and was considered a staple of the ancient Greek diet. Unlike so many cultivated plants that have lost their nutritional value from years of genetic manipulation, kale has held remarkably true to its original varieties, making it one of the healthiest greens around. Dark-green leafy veggies are exceptionally high in carotenoids, including zeaxanthin and lutein, powerful antioxidants that protect us from disease. The fresher the kale, the better it is. As soon as kale is harvested, it begins to oxidate and lose its potent nutrients. Kale is relatively easy to grow in your backyard; in fact, it's so hardy that most farmers grow it, and farmers markets carry it year-round.

SERVES 4

6 cups chopped kale

3 cups finely sliced Brussels sprouts

2 small avocados, cut into cubes

Juice of 1 large lemon

½ teaspoon flaky sea salt

½ cup extra-virgin olive oil

Combine the kale, Brussels sprouts, and avocado in a large salad bowl.

Combine the lemon juice and salt in a small bowl. Slowly add the olive oil while whisking with a fork to emulsify.

Pour the dressing over the salad and toss well to combine before serving.

BEET SALAD

I have experimented with cooking beets many different ways and I always get the best result by baking them in salt. To do this, you have to bury the beets in more than 2 pounds of coarse sea salt and bake them for 90 minutes. The resulting beets are perfectly seasoned—all that salt doesn't permeate them—and have a firm yet yielding texture. These sweet beets go well with creamy whipped goat cheese and a sprinkle of caraway seeds to add a bit of crunch.

SERVES 4

2 to 3 pounds coarse sea salt, enough to cover the beets

3 medium beets, scrubbed and tops removed

4 ounces goat cheese

½ teaspoon fine sea salt

5 tablespoons extra-virgin olive oil

Freshly ground black pepper

1 tablespoon caraway seeds

1 tablespoon balsamic vinegar

4 cups arugula

Preheat the oven to 350°F. Pour a layer of coarse sea salt over the bottom of an 8-by-4-inch loaf pan.

Place the beets in the pan and fill with coarse sea salt until the beets are covered.

Bake for 1 hour 30 minutes. Test for doneness by sliding a paring knife into one of the beets. When the knife meets little resistance, the beets are done. When they're cool enough to handle, brush off and discard all the salt. Peel the beets and cut each one into 8 segments.

In a large bowl, whip the goat cheese, fine sea salt, 2 tablespoons of the olive oil, and the pepper with a fork.

Toast the caraway seeds in a small dry skillet over medium-high heat, stirring with a wooden spoon until fragrant, 2 or 3 minutes. Put the toasted seeds in a salad bowl and mix with the vinegar and the remaining 3 tablespoons olive oil. Set aside a tablespoon of this dressing.

Add the arugula to the bowl and toss to coat with the dressing. Add the beets and mix in the reserved salad dressing. Top with the whipped goat cheese and serve.

TWENTY-FOUR-HOUR ONION SOUP

When you make onion soup in a slow cooker, the flavor becomes intense—especially when you cook it for 24 hours. First, you create the broth and leave it overnight in the slow cooker. The resulting beef stock is rich in vitamins and minerals including calcium, magnesium, and phosphorus. It promotes strong, healthy bones and is good for your digestion and immune system. In the morning, you add the rest of the ingredients and let everything simmer together all day on low heat. Your deeply flavored soup will be ready by dinnertime. Top each serving with crusty bread and a slice of cheese and broil until bubbly before digging in.

SERVES 8

2 to 3 pounds grass-fed beef bones (see Note)

3 carrots, coarsely chopped

3 celery stalks, coarsely chopped

1 large onion, coarsely chopped

2 bay leaves

5 garlic cloves

Fine sea salt

2 tablespoons ghee (see page 24)

6 large yellow onions, sliced

2 tablespoons all-purpose flour

½ cup dry white wine

8 slices crusty bread

8 slices Gruyère cheese

SPECIAL EQUIPMENT
Slow cooker

Preheat the oven to 350°F. Place the beef bones in a large roasting pan and cook them until well browned, about 30 minutes.

Place the bones in the slow cooker.

Deglaze the roasting pan with ¼ cup hot water; use a wooden spoon to scrape off the parts that stick. Add this flavorful water to the slow cooker along with the carrots, celery, onion, bay leaves, and garlic. Fill the slow cooker with water. Set the temperature to low and leave it overnight, about 12 hours.

In the morning, strain the broth through a large colander, discarding any solid pieces. Turn off the heat and let the broth cool down. The stock will set like gelatin and the fat will rise to the top and harden. Skim the fat off. Taste the broth; season with salt to taste. Pour 10 cups of stock back into the slow cooker. (Refrigerate the remaining stock in an airtight container for up to 4 days, or freeze for up to 6 months.)

Melt the butter in a large sauté pan over medium heat. Add the onions and sauté, stirring frequently, until they brown, about 20 minutes. Add the flour to the onions. Cook, stirring with a wooden spoon, for about 1 minute. Deglaze the pan with the white wine. Add 1 tablespoon salt and cook for 1 minute, then add the mixture to the slow cooker.

With the slow cooker still on low, cook until the onions are very soft, about 8 hours.

Before serving, preheat the oven to 400°F. Arrange bread slices in a single layer on a baking sheet and bake until crispy, about 10 minutes. Divide the soup between individual ovenproof bowls. Float a slice of the crispy bread in each soup bowl and top with a thick slice of Gruyère cheese. Set the oven to broil and broil until the cheese is golden brown, about 3 minutes. Serve hot.

NOTE

You can pick up grass-fed beef bones at your local farm or butcher shop.

BOILED ARTICHOKES

The artichoke is a daunting-looking food; it's a thistle, after all. However, at its heart lies a real culinary treat. To get there, you begin by pulling off the outermost petals, one at a time. The lower end of the petal is edible and, after dipping it in vinaigrette, you scrape the fleshy part off with your teeth. At the center of the artichoke, you'll find translucent leaves and a hairy center (the choke), which you remove with a spoon. Below this lies the heart. Cut it into bite-sized pieces and dip into the vinaigrette for a delicious reward.

SERVES 4

ARTICHOKES
4 artichokes
2 bay leaves
2 lemons, cut in half
2 garlic cloves
2 tablespoons coarse sea salt

VINAIGRETTE
¼ cup white wine vinegar
2 tablespoons Dijon mustard
½ cup olive oil
1 hard-cooked large pasture-raised egg
2 tablespoons finely chopped fresh flat-leaf parsley
Flaky sea salt and freshly ground black pepper

Pull off any smaller, tough leaves toward the base and on the stem of the artichokes.

Place the artichokes in a heavy pot. Cover with 4 quarts water. Add the bay leaves, squeeze in the juice of the lemons, then drop the squeezed lemon halves into the water and add the garlic and salt to the pot. Cover the pot.

Bring to a boil and cook until a knife inserted into the artichokes gives no resistance, about 20 minutes. Turn off the heat and let the artichokes steep in the water for 5 to 10 minutes.

Meanwhile, combine the vinegar and mustard in a small bowl. Slowly add the olive oil while whisking with a fork.

Cut the hard-boiled egg in half, and press each half through a sieve into the vinaigrette. Add the parsley and salt and pepper to taste.

Lift the artichokes out of the water and turn them upside down in a colander to drain.

Serve the artichokes hot or at room temperature with the vinaigrette for dipping on the side.

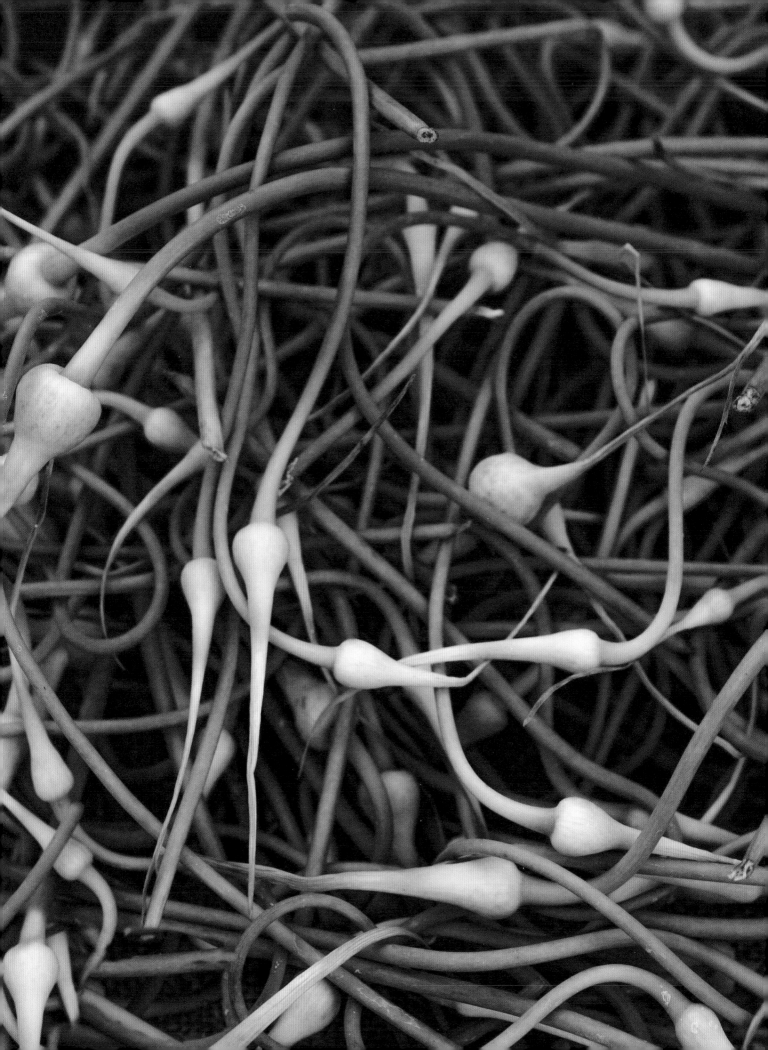

GARLIC SCAPE COMPOUND BUTTER

Garlic scapes are the green stems that grow from garlic roots in late spring. They are milder in taste than garlic cloves, and they're delicious when you mix them into butter. The butter can be eaten on some crusty bread sprinkled with coarse salt. It's also great on steaks, fish, vegetables, and baked or mashed potatoes.

Garlic scape season is very short, so when I find them at the market, I usually make a larger quantity of the butter and freeze some.

MAKES 1 CUP

1 cup cultured unsalted butter (see page 22), at room temperature
4 large garlic scapes, finely chopped

Place the butter in a large bowl and mash it with a potato masher. Add the chopped garlic scapes and continue to mash until fully incorporated.

Place a large piece of foil on your counter and top with an equally long layer of parchment paper. Scoop the mixed butter on top of the parchment. Use the parchment to roll and shape the butter into a cylinder or log. Wrap the log in the parchment and foil and refrigerate it.

The butter will keep for about 1 week in the refrigerator and for 1 month in the freezer.

ZUCCHINI TART

This tart is delicious at room temperature, making it a great picnic food. The dough for the tart can be made up to a week in advance and kept in the refrigerator. It also freezes well. With the dough on hand, this tart comes together very fast: simply slice the zucchini, combine the cheese with the herbs, spread the cheese mixture over the flattened dough, top with the zucchini, and shape it into a rustic free-form tart before baking.

MAKES ONE 11- TO 12-INCH TART; SERVES 4 TO 6

1 large zucchini, thinly sliced

Flaky sea salt

Savory Tart Dough (page 247)

8 ounces goat cheese

1 tablespoon finely chopped fresh chives

⅛ teaspoon finely grated lemon zest

1 teaspoon fresh lemon juice

1 teaspoon chopped fresh rosemary

¼ cup grated Parmesan cheese

Freshly ground black pepper

Extra-virgin olive oil

Place the zucchini slices in a strainer and sprinkle them evenly with ½ teaspoon salt. Let drain for 30 minutes, then spread them out on paper towels to drain for another 30 minutes.

When the zucchini has almost finished draining, preheat the oven to 350°F.

Transfer the tart dough to a baking sheet.

Using a potato masher, mash together the goat cheese, chives, lemon zest, lemon juice, rosemary, Parmesan, a pinch of salt, and pepper to taste in a small bowl.

Flour your hands and gently pull and stretch the dough into a 13- to 14-inch circle on the baking sheet.

Spread the cheese mixture over the crust, leaving a 2-inch border all around. Starting at the outside edge, layer the zucchini, overlapping the slices on top of the cheese mixture. Drizzle with olive oil.

Fold the border of the dough over the filling. Bake until the crust is golden brown, 40 to 45 minutes.

TOMATO TART

This tart makes great use of sun-ripened, fresh-off-the-vine tomatoes, so when your garden is overflowing with them, reach for this recipe. The dough is shaped into a free-form crust, making a beautiful rustic tart.

MAKES ONE 11- TO 12-INCH TART; SERVES 4 TO 6

Savory Tart Dough (page 247)
4 medium tomatoes, cut into thin slices, or 1 pint cherry tomatoes, cut in half
1 tablespoon flaky sea salt
1 tablespoon extra-virgin olive oil, plus more for drizzling
1 medium onion, thinly sliced
All-purpose flour, for shaping the crust
Leaves from 2 fresh thyme sprigs

Preheat the oven to 350°F.

Spread the tomato slices out over several layers of paper towels. Sprinkle them evenly with the salt and let drain for 30 minutes.

Meanwhile, coat a medium sauté pan with the olive oil and sauté the onion, stirring occasionally, until soft and sweet, about 8 minutes.

Put the Savory Tart Dough on a baking sheet.

Lightly flour your hands and gently pull and stretch the dough into a 13- to 14-inch circle.

Spread the onions over the dough, leaving a 2-inch border.

Arrange the tomatoes over the onions; there should be no onions visible when all the tomatoes have been layered on top. Drizzle with the olive oil and top with the thyme sprigs.

Fold the border of the dough over the filling. Bake until the crust is golden brown, 40 to 45 minutes.

This tart can be served hot out of the oven but is just as delicious at room temperature. Keep leftovers covered in the refrigerator for up to 4 days or freeze for up to 2 months. Bring back to room temperature before serving or reheat in the oven.

SUN-DRIED TOMATOES

Whenever farm-fresh sun-ripened tomatoes are in season, it is easy to grow or buy more than you can eat. When you have extra, try turning them into sun-dried tomatoes. They are delicious as a snack or can be added to a salad, a pasta dish, or a sandwich, and you can use them to flavor sauces, dips, and dressings. They are so versatile, I even freeze them to have year-round.

The ideal conditions for true sun-drying outdoors are warm temperatures, low humidity, and a constant breeze. But watching the tomatoes dry and tasting their concentrated flavor is worth trying no matter where you live. If it doesn't work well in your climate, you can always use the oven or a dehydrator (see Variations).

MAKES ABOUT 2 CUPS

5 pounds tomatoes
2 teaspoons flaky sea salt

Cut the tomatoes into ¼-inch-thick slices, about 4 slices per tomato. Sprinkle them with the salt.

To dry the tomatoes in the sun, arrange them in a single layer on perforated trays, racks, or stainless steel screens. Raise them off the ground by placing the trays on blocks or bricks to allow air to circulate underneath. Cover the trays with protective netting or cheesecloth and place in direct sunlight. After sundown or if the weather changes, bring the trays inside and then outside again the following day.

When dried, the tomatoes should be pliable but not brittle. In perfect dry weather conditions, it takes 4 to 7 days to dry the tomatoes. Store the dried tomatoes in an airtight container in the refrigerator for up to 18 months.

VARIATIONS

To dry tomatoes in the oven: Preheat the oven to 200°F, or the lowest setting possible. Arrange the tomatoes on an oven rack and bake for 6 to 10 hours, depending on thickness. (Place a baking sheet on a lower rack to catch juices as the tomatoes dry.) When done, the tomatoes should be pliable but not brittle.

To dry tomatoes in a dehydrator: Arrange the tomatoes cut side up on the dehydrator rack. Set the temperature to 135°F. Check on the tomatoes after about 8 hours; depending on the thickness of the slices, they should take approximately 12 hours to dry.

CRISPY ROASTED POTATOES

To make the crispiest potatoes, boil them first and then roast them. This extra step gives the potatoes the most delicious crust. Using duck fat (if you have it!) adds crunch as well as great flavor.

SERVES 4

2 pounds Yukon Gold potatoes, cut into bite-sized cubes
2 tablespoons coarse sea salt
1 tablespoon duck fat or extra-virgin olive oil

Place the potatoes in a medium pot, cover with 2 quarts water, and add the salt. Bring to a boil over high heat, then reduce the heat and simmer until the potatoes are tender, about 10 minutes.

Drain the potatoes into a colander. Shake the colander back and forth to scuff them up.

Preheat the oven to 350°F.

Brush the potatoes with duck fat or drizzle with olive oil. Bake until crisp and golden, about 1 hour 10 minutes.

RÖSTI

Rösti is a traditional Swiss dish made from grated potatoes. It has its origins as the breakfast dish of the farmers of eastern Switzerland, but nowadays it's often eaten as a side dish and can be found on menus everywhere in Switzerland as well as other parts of the world. You can fry this potato pancake in a combination of duck fat and butter for a crispy texture and rich flavor, or if duck fat is unavailable, use ghee. I like to top rösti with a fried egg to make a satisfying breakfast.

SERVES 4

2 large russet potatoes, scrubbed but unpeeled

Flaky sea salt and freshly ground black pepper

4 tablespoons unsalted butter

2 tablespoons duck fat or ghee (see page 24), plus more to fry the eggs

4 large pasture-raised eggs

Place the whole potatoes in a Dutch oven or other large heavy pot, cover with water, and add a pinch of salt. Bring to a boil over medium-high heat; reduce the heat to low and simmer the potatoes until just tender, about 30 minutes. Drain and chill for at least 4 hours (see Note).

Coarsely grate the potatoes into a large bowl and season with salt and pepper. Divide into 4 servings.

Over medium-high heat, melt 1½ teaspoons of the butter and ¾ teaspoon of the duck fat in a 6-inch skillet.

Add one portion of the grated potato. Press with a spatula to form a flat cake. Do not stir. Occasionally shake the pan to loosen the potato. Cook on one side until crisp and browned, about 10 minutes. Slide the rösti onto a plate.

Add another 1½ teaspoons of the butter and ¾ teaspoon of the duck fat to the pan. Put a plate on top of the rösti to flip it over and slide it back into the pan. Continue cooking until the bottom is browned and the potatoes are tender in the middle when poked with a knife, another 6 to 8 minutes.

Repeat with the remaining potato cakes, cooking one at a time.

Coat a skillet with ghee, and fry the eggs sunny-side up.

To serve, top each potato cake with a fried egg.

NOTE

Chilling the potatoes before grating them helps them hold together.

VARIATION

If making one big rösti, melt 1 tablespoon of the butter and ½ tablespoon of the duck fat in a 10-inch pan and add all of the grated potato. Cook for about 10 minutes, until the underside is crisp and browned, then slide the rösti onto a plate. Return the pan to the heat and add another tablespoon butter and ½ tablespoon fat. Put a plate on top of the rösti to flip it over and slide it back into the pan. Cook for about 8 more minutes, until the bottom is crisp and browned.

STEWED PEARS

Usually fruit is stewed with lots of sugar, but in this recipe the pear gets stewed in fresh-pressed apple juice, making it a sugar-free treat that is healthy and wholesome. The stewed pear is great by itself or as a topping for oatmeal (see page 226), plain yogurt (see page 19), or muesli (see page 233). Juice fresh apples to stew the pears or buy raw fresh organic juice—ideally cold pressed or high-pressure processed (HPP).

SERVES 4

4 pears, such as Bosc, peeled, quartered, and cored
1 apple, freshly juiced using a juicer, or ½ cup raw organic juice
¼ teaspoon vanilla extract or ½ vanilla bean

Combine the pears, apple juice, and vanilla in a small saucepan. (If using a vanilla bean, scrape the seeds into the pan and add the pods.) Stew until the pears are soft, about 15 minutes.

Store leftovers in an airtight container in the refrigerator for up to 3 days.

PEAR CRISP

A warm crisp tastes as indulgent as a slice of pie, and yet it's so much easier and faster to make. I love the combination of nuts and the sweet juice from the pears in the topping. You can make this crisp with any fruit that is in season, such as apples, berries, plums, peaches, or even cherries. And pecans or almonds are fine substitutes for the walnuts. I like to serve the crisp warm in ramekins, topped with a scoop of vanilla ice cream.

SERVES 4

⅓ cup home-milled soft white wheat flour (see page 224) or organic whole wheat pastry flour (see Resources, page 264)

¼ cup rolled oats (not quick-cooking)

3 tablespoons light brown sugar

1 teaspoon ground cinnamon

⅛ teaspoon fine sea salt

4 tablespoons (½ stick) cold unsalted butter, cut into small pieces, plus more for coating the ramekins

½ cup walnuts, roughly chopped

4 pears, peeled, cored, and cut into small dice (about 2 cups)

Vanilla Ice Cream (page 55), for serving

Preheat the oven to 350°F.

Combine the flour, oats, brown sugar, cinnamon, and salt in a large bowl.

Add the butter to the dry ingredients and lightly knead with your hands until the mixture forms coarse crumbs. Mix in the walnuts.

Coat four 4-inch ramekins with butter and fill with the diced pears. Sprinkle each ramekin with a quarter of the flour mixture.

Bake until the topping is golden brown, about 45 minutes. Serve warm with a scoop of vanilla ice cream on top.

SLOW-COOKED APPLESAUCE

Once you've made your own applesauce, you'll wonder why you haven't always done so. It tastes better, is healthier, and can be eaten at breakfast, lunch, or dinner. It's great by itself, spooned over oatmeal (see page 226), mixed with yogurt (see page 19), or used as a condiment. This recipe makes about 3 cups, but you can also make it in larger batches and freeze it. Use any kind of apple or try a combination.

When making baked goods, you can use applesauce to replace liquid fats at a one-to-one ratio. In addition, when using this applesauce in the batter for cookies or cakes, you can reduce the sugar because the apples are filled with natural sweetness.

MAKES ABOUT 3 CUPS

8 apples, peeled, cored, and cut into chunks
2 dates, pitted
2 cinnamon sticks

SPECIAL EQUIPMENT
Slow cooker

Combine the apples, dates, and cinnamon sticks in the slow cooker. Cover and cook on low for about 7 hours, stirring every couple of hours.

Serve warm, or allow to cool and transfer to a closed container. Refrigerate for up to 10 days or freeze for up to 1 year.

MULLED APPLE CIDER

This wholesome recipe uses fresh apples and spices and is not only great for warming up your entire family after a fall or winter day spent outdoors, but will also fill your home with that same wonderful warm and spicy fragrance you get when you bake an apple pie.

SERVES 9 TO 12

12 apples (any kind will do), cut into quarters (no need to peel or core them)
⅓ cup raw honey, or more to taste
4 cinnamon sticks
1 tablespoon whole cloves
1 whole nutmeg
Zest of 1 lemon, removed in strips (avoid the white part as much as possible)
Rum (optional)

Place the apple quarters, honey, cinnamon sticks, cloves, nutmeg, and lemon zest in a Dutch oven or other large heavy pot. Fill with just enough water to cover the apples.

Leaving the pot uncovered, bring to a boil over medium-high heat. Reduce the heat and simmer uncovered for 45 minutes, until the apples are so soft they can be mashed with the back of a fork.

Turn off the heat and mash the apples with a potato masher.

Strain the cider through a fine-mesh sieve into a big bowl, forcing out some of the juice. Don't push it all through as the cider may get too thick. Discard the fruit pulp and spices.

The cider can be stored, covered, in the refrigerator for up to 1 week. Reheat in a pot if you want to serve it warm. For a grown-up drink, add a splash of rum before serving.

PEACH MARMALADE

This all-natural marmalade isn't loaded with sugar and pectin powder. The recipe uses the cooked-down juice of green apples as the natural thickening agent, and the flavor of the apples doesn't interfere with the flavor of the peaches. The apples are also a fast coagulant, which means less boiling time and more retained vitamins in the finished product. Peaches are a great fruit for turning into marmalade, but berries would work well, too.

This recipe makes only a small batch. My family devours it, still warm, with fresh crusty bread (see page 243) and homemade butter (see page 22). You can increase the quantities and preserve your marmalade. For more information on sterilizing and preparing a canning bath, check out the Resources (page 264).

MAKES ABOUT 1 CUP

6 Granny Smith apples, unpeeled, cut into cubes (about 6 cups; include the cores)

Juice of ½ lemon

6 ripe peaches, unpeeled, cut into cubes (about 6 cups)

⅓ cup honey, or more to taste, depending on the sweetness of the fruit

Combine the apples and lemon juice in a medium pot. Add 1 quart water. Cover, place over high heat, and boil for 40 minutes.

Strain the juice through a sieve and discard the pulp. Return the juice to the pot, set over high heat, and boil for 10 minutes.

Add the peaches and honey and cook over high heat for about 20 minutes. To test if the marmalade is done, drop a spoonful onto a plate. As it cools, you can see if it has reached the thick consistency of marmalade. If it is too thin, let it boil down for a few more minutes and then check again.

Pour the marmalade into a jar, let cool, and secure the lid. It will keep for about 2 weeks in the refrigerator.

PEACH TART

You don't even need a tart pan to make this peach tart; simply fold the dough around the fruit.

SERVES 4

½ cup Almond Paste (recipe follows)

1 large pasture-raised egg

2 large ripe peaches, unpeeled, thinly sliced

1 teaspoon arrowroot powder or cornstarch

1 teaspoon raw honey, or more to taste, depending on the sweetness of the fruit

⅛ teaspoon fine sea salt

½ vanilla bean

Sweet Tart Dough (page 249)

Preheat the oven to 350°F. Line a baking sheet with parchment paper.

Place the almond paste in a medium bowl and add the egg. Mix well with a large spoon.

In another medium bowl, combine the peach slices with the arrowroot, honey, and salt. Split the vanilla bean in half lengthwise and scrape the seeds into the bowl with the peaches. Discard the bean.

Transfer the tart dough to the prepared baking sheet. Lightly flour your hands and gently pull and stretch the dough into a 13- to 14-inch circle. You can also divide the dough into 4 pieces, shaping each into a 3½-inch circle, to create individual tarts.

Spread the almond paste mixture over the dough, leaving a 2-inch border all around. Arrange the fruit in concentric circles over the almond paste. Fold the edges of the dough over the filling.

Bake until the crust is golden brown, 30 to 40 minutes. Serve warm or at room temperature. Leftovers can be kept for up to 1 day at room temperature or for up to 5 days in the refrigerator.

continued

ALMOND PASTE

MAKES ABOUT 1 CUP

1 cup blanched almonds (see Note)
¹/₃ cup organic cane sugar
1 tablespoon raw honey
1 teaspoon almond extract

Place the almonds in a food processor and grind into a powder. Add the sugar, honey, and almond extract and blend until a paste forms.

Keep leftovers in an airtight container in the refrigerator for up to 3 months or in the freezer for up to 1 year. Bring to room temperature before using.

NOTE

To blanch almonds, boil them for 1 minute, then rinse with cold water. Rub the skins off with your fingers.

PLUM COBBLER

Serve cobbler warm right out of the oven and add a scoop of ice cream for a delicious summer treat.

SERVES 4

FRUIT

8 cups thinly sliced peeled plums (about 24 plums)

2 tablespoons raw honey

2 teaspoons arrowroot powder or cornstarch

1 teaspoon lemon juice

½ teaspoon ground cinnamon

TOPPING

¾ cup home-milled soft white wheat flour (see page 224) or organic whole wheat pastry flour (see Resources, page 264)

4 tablespoons raw sugar

1½ tablespoons organic cane sugar

¾ teaspoon baking powder

½ teaspoon fine sea salt

4 tablespoons (½ stick) unsalted butter, cut into small pieces, plus more for coating the baking dish

1½ teaspoons ground cinnamon

Vanilla ice cream, for serving (optional)

Preheat the oven to 425°F.

Combine the plums, honey, arrowroot, lemon juice, and cinnamon in a large bowl. Toss gently until well mixed.

Transfer to an 8-by-10-inch buttered baking dish. Bake for 10 minutes.

Meanwhile, combine the flour, 3 tablespoons of the raw sugar, the cane sugar, baking powder, salt, and butter in a medium bowl. Mix together by hand until the mixture resembles coarse crumbs. Stir in 2 tablespoons water until the crumbs start to clump together.

Remove the plums from the oven. Drop large spoonfuls of the batter over the fruit.

Combine the remaining tablespoon raw sugar with the cinnamon in a small bowl and sprinkle the mixture over the cobbler.

Bake until the top just begins to brown, 10 to 15 minutes. Reduce the heat to 350°F and cook until the fruit juices are thickened and bubbly, another 35 to 40 minutes. If the topping starts to get too brown, cover it with parchment paper. Serve warm, topped with vanilla ice cream if desired. Leftovers can be kept covered in the refrigerator for up to 5 days.

CLAFOUTIS

Clafoutis is the dessert to make to impress your guests. It looks sophisticated, but it comes together quickly with a simple batter and most any fruit. This classic French dessert is traditionally made with cherries, and if you substitute plums, grapes, or pears for the cherries, the French name changes also, from clafoutis to *flaugnarde*.

SERVES 4

2 tablespoons unsalted butter, melted, plus more butter, at room temperature, for greasing the pan

2½ cups cherries, pitted

¼ cup plus 1 teaspoon raw honey

1 teaspoon arrowroot powder or cornstarch

½ cup home-milled soft white wheat flour (see page 224) or organic whole wheat pastry flour (see Resources, page 264)

4 large pasture-raised eggs

1 cup whole milk (ideally raw or nonhomogenized grass-fed)

1 teaspoon vanilla extract

½ teaspoon almond extract

¼ teaspoon fine sea salt

Preheat the oven to 400°F. Butter a heavy skillet or a 9-inch cake pan.

In a large bowl, toss the cherries with the 1 teaspoon honey and the arrowroot. Spread the mixture evenly in the buttered skillet.

Combine the ¼ cup honey, the flour, eggs, milk, melted butter, vanilla, almond extract, and salt in a food processor and blend for a couple of seconds to combine. Pour the batter over the cherries.

Bake until firm and golden, about 50 minutes.

You can serve clafoutis directly from the skillet. It is best served lukewarm. Leftovers can be kept covered at room temperature for up to 12 hours or for up to 3 days in the refrigerator.

INTO
THE
WILD

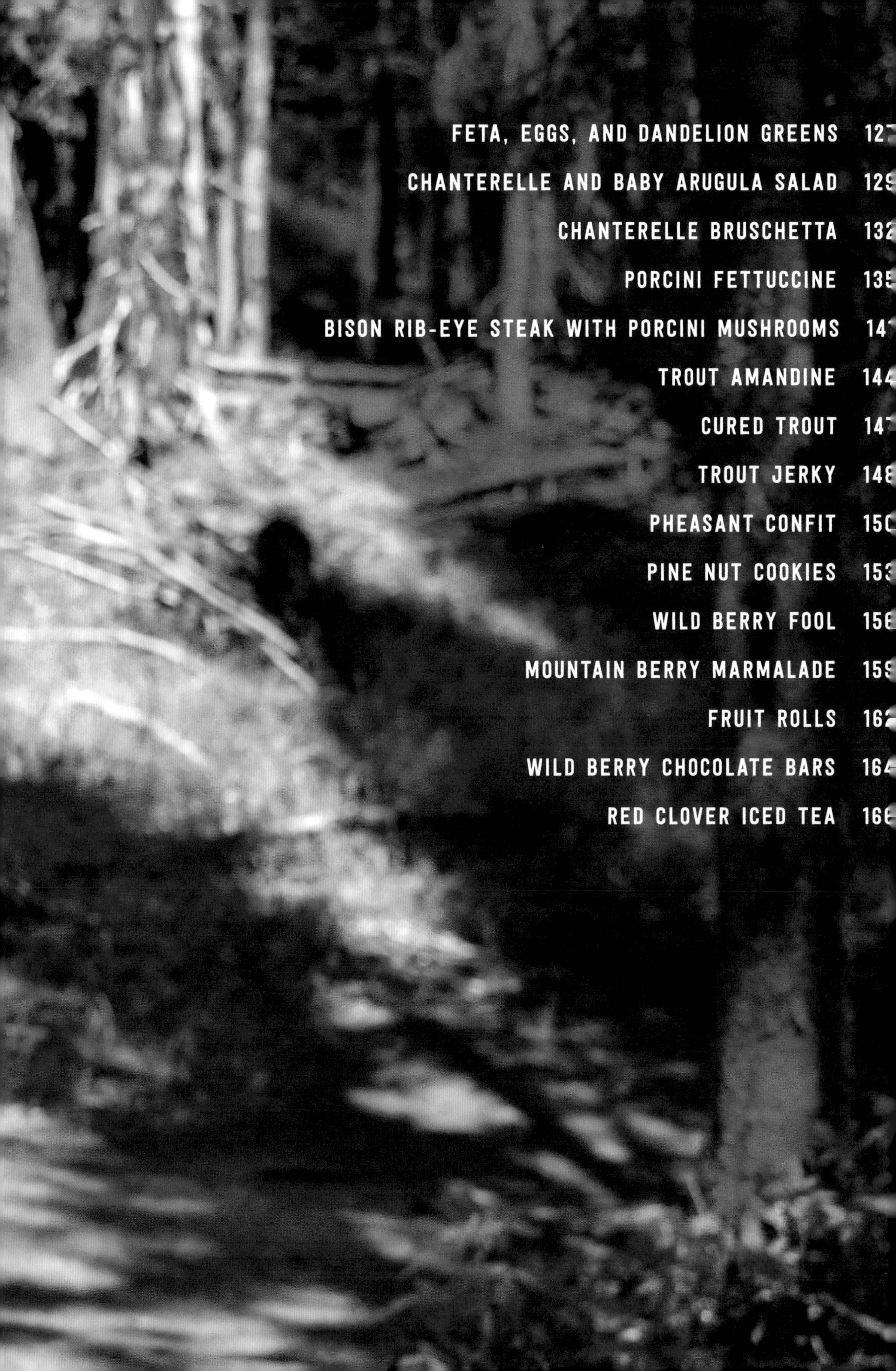

FETA, EGGS, AND DANDELION GREENS 127

CHANTERELLE AND BABY ARUGULA SALAD 129

CHANTERELLE BRUSCHETTA 132

PORCINI FETTUCCINE 135

BISON RIB-EYE STEAK WITH PORCINI MUSHROOMS 141

TROUT AMANDINE 144

CURED TROUT 147

TROUT JERKY 148

PHEASANT CONFIT 150

PINE NUT COOKIES 153

WILD BERRY FOOL 156

MOUNTAIN BERRY MARMALADE 159

FRUIT ROLLS 162

WILD BERRY CHOCOLATE BARS 164

RED CLOVER ICED TEA 166

The lover of nature is he who has retained the spirit of infancy even into the era of manhood.

—RALPH WALDO EMERSON, *NATURE*

I'll never forget the first time Nate King, the chef at Cache Cache in Aspen, took me foraging. There is a big difference between hiking to a destination, like a cabin or a peak, and walking while searching for food hidden in the undergrowth. Looking specifically for mushrooms, knife in hand, feels elemental, and my senses are instantly engaged by the smell of Douglas firs, the rustling of leaves, and the crunching of pine needles under my feet. Nate has, over the years, developed an intuitive sense for finding mushrooms, and he passed those skills on to me. Searching, smelling, and listening is a grounding experience that puts me right in the moment, and I find myself with an acute alertness to my environment, a sort of animal instinct I'd never experienced before.

On our first foraging trip, we went deep into the forest and, even though Nate kept saying that all the signs were there, we never found any mushrooms and gave up. Then, on the way back, I spotted a patch, and I celebrated my discovery as if I'd solved world hunger!

The second time I went foraging, my husband, Chad, and I drove with the kids all the way up Larkspur Mountain and entered the forest via a barely distinguishable trail. There were edible flowers and berries along the way, which we ate straight off the bushes as we headed toward a group of fallen trees. Soon we found the first mushroom, and as Hendrix ran deeper into the forest, climbing over branches, roots, and rocks, he suddenly cried out: "Dad! Mom! Come quickly!"

I was afraid he'd spotted a bear cub, but instead he pointed at an enormous porcini mushroom. We let him cut it out of the ground with his own knife, which, he later confessed, made him feel nervous but also grown up. Liloo tried pulling the mushrooms with her hands. I think I was more excited than all of them. The possibilities of these mushrooms were endless: on the drive home, I dreamed of steak with porcini, pasta with porcini, and a simple mushroom bruschetta.

When learning how to forage, go with experts at first and join foraging seminars. Field experience is the best way to learn. Also buy field guides and use several different ones to cross-reference information. Concentrate on a few species and expand your list once you become more confident. I started out with porcini, chanterelle, wood ear, and oyster mushrooms—all of which are easily identifiable. Treat everything else as suspicious. If you are not 100 percent sure, show your collection to an expert to verify what you've found. Many species have poisonous look-alikes, so don't ever eat a mushroom unless you are certain of what it is.

The rule of making a positive identification before picking and eating also applies to berries. Foraging for berries is different from finding mushrooms since berries can grow randomly in parks and gardens and by roads as well as on nature trails and in the woods. I have found everything from thimbleberries and serviceberries to blackberries, blueberries, and raspberries. We eat them as we walk and gather them for dessert, turn them into fruit rolls or marmalade, or use them in chocolate bars. When we eat them later, the flavor takes us back to our foraging adventure.

For recommended readings on foraging, see Resources (page 264).

FETA, EGGS, AND DANDELION GREENS

Dandelion greens are very nutritious: they are high in calcium, rich in iron, and loaded with antioxidants. They are best harvested in springtime when the young greens are still tender and their flavor is mild. But blanching them in boiling water first will remove some of their bitterness. Cultivated dandelions from the store are less bitter than wild ones, but in both cases it's best to taste test them first. If you're foraging your own, be careful not to gather them in areas that have been sprayed with pesticide.

SERVES 4

4 cups chopped dandelion greens, thick stems removed

2 tablespoons ghee (see page 24)

1 leek, white and light green parts only, finely chopped

4 large pasture-raised eggs

¼ cup crumbled feta cheese

Bring a large pot of water to a boil. Add the dandelion greens and blanch for 1 to 2 minutes. Drain the greens thoroughly, patting them as dry as possible with paper towels.

Melt the ghee in a 10-inch sauté pan set over medium heat. Sauté the leeks in the ghee until tender, about 5 minutes. Add the dandelion greens one handful at a time. Cook each handful until wilted, then add more.

When all the greens are wilted, crack the eggs into the pan on top of the greens. Top with feta cheese and cook uncovered until the whites of the eggs are set, about 5 minutes.

CHANTERELLE AND BABY ARUGULA SALAD

When your ingredients are fresh and full of personality, there is very little you need to do to prepare a great dish. Here, you just lightly sauté the chanterelle mushrooms to bring out their flavor. Serve them warm on top of fresh-picked arugula.

SERVES 4

4 tablespoons extra-virgin olive oil

1 tablespoon unsalted butter

2 cups bite-sized pieces chanterelle mushrooms

1 tablespoon chopped shallot

1 garlic clove, crushed

¾ teaspoon chopped fresh thyme

Fine sea salt and freshly ground black pepper

1 tablespoon plus 2½ teaspoons lemon juice

4 cups baby arugula

¼ cup pecorino, shaved with a vegetable peeler

Heat 1 tablespoon of the olive oil and the butter in a large skillet over medium heat until the butter has melted.

Add the mushrooms. Stirring often, let them sear until browned, about 10 minutes. Add the shallot, garlic, and thyme and sauté, stirring often, until the liquid from the mushrooms has evaporated, about 5 more minutes. The edges should be crispy and the texture firm. Season the mushrooms with salt and pepper to taste and add 1½ teaspoons of the lemon juice.

To make the dressing, put the remaining 1 tablespoon plus 1 teaspoon lemon juice in a small bowl and slowly pour in the remaining 3 tablespoons olive oil while whisking with a fork. Season with salt and pepper to taste.

Place the arugula in a large bowl. Pour the dressing over it and toss well to combine. Add the warm sautéed mushrooms and top with the shaved pecorino.

CHANTERELLE BRUSCHETTA

Chanterelles look like golden flowers popping out of the grassy, mossy forest floor. Once you find them, note your spot. They'll grow back in the same place every year, which makes them easier to find than most other mushrooms. Use a brush or a damp towel to clean them well before using them.

SERVES 4

1 tablespoon extra-virgin olive oil

1 tablespoon unsalted butter

2 cups bite-sized pieces chanterelle mushrooms

1 tablespoon chopped shallot

1 garlic clove, crushed

¾ teaspoon chopped fresh thyme

Salt and freshly ground black pepper

1½ teaspoons lemon juice

4 slices of crusty artisan bread, toasted

¼ cup Parmesan, shaved with a vegetable peeler

Heat the olive oil and butter in a large skillet over medium heat until the butter has melted. Add the mushrooms. Stirring often, let them sear until browned, about 10 minutes. Add the shallot, garlic, and thyme and sauté, stirring often, until the liquid from the mushrooms has evaporated, about 5 more minutes. The edges should be crispy and the texture firm.

Season the mushrooms with salt and pepper to taste and add the lemon juice.

To serve, divide the mushrooms among the pieces of toast and top with shaved Parmesan.

PORCINI FETTUCCINE

Porcini mushrooms are difficult to cultivate, so take advantage when these mushrooms are in season, which is autumn in the Northern Hemisphere. During the height of the season, I take a couple of foraging trips into the woods and usually end up with more than I can eat. So I dry them, which keeps the porcini's intense aroma and flavor intact. You can slice them and dry them in a dehydrator or in the sun. The dried porcini add a deep woodsy flavor to this pasta recipe, and you can enjoy it all year long.

SERVES 4

1½ cups dried porcini mushrooms (recipe follows)

2 tablespoons extra-virgin olive oil

4 whole garlic cloves

½ cup white wine

10 sage leaves, chopped

1 cup chicken broth

½ teaspoon fine sea salt

3 tablespoons unsalted butter

12 ounces fettuccine pasta

½ cup grated Parmesan

Place the mushrooms in a medium bowl and cover with 2 cups warm water. Soak for 15 minutes. Carefully remove the mushrooms and reserve 1 cup of the soaking liquid. If the mushrooms are gritty, pour the soaking liquid through a coffee filter to remove the grit.

Heat the olive oil in a large sauté pan over medium heat. Add the garlic and sauté for 3 minutes. Remove the cloves and discard.

Add the rehydrated mushrooms to the same pan and cook until soft, about 2 minutes. Raise the temperature to high and add the wine and sage. Cook, stirring occasionally, until the alcohol evaporates, about 3 minutes.

Add the broth, reserved mushroom water, and salt. Continue to cook over high heat until almost all the liquid has evaporated, about 20 minutes. Turn off the heat and swirl in the butter.

While the broth reduces, bring a large pot of salted water to a boil and cook the fettuccine until al dente. Drain the pasta and toss to combine with the mushroom mixture. Serve with grated Parmesan on top. Leftovers can be kept in an airtight container in the refrigerator for up to 3 days.

continued

HOME-DRIED PORCINI MUSHROOMS

To dry mushrooms in a dehydrator, place sliced porcinis on the drying rack in a single layer. Set the temperature to 120°F. They should be ready in 18 to 24 hours. When done, the mushrooms should be so dry that they can be cracked in half.

To dry mushrooms in the sun, place them on racks or stainless steel screens. Raise them off the ground by placing the racks on blocks or bricks; this will allow air to circulate underneath. Cover the racks with protective netting or cheesecloth and place in direct sunlight. After sundown or if the weather changes, bring them indoors. Bring the racks out in the sun the next day. When done, the mushrooms should be so dry that they can be cracked in half. In ideal conditions, this will take about 1 week.

BISON RIB-EYE STEAK WITH PORCINI MUSHROOMS

Freshly picked porcini are the true stars of this dish. The bison steaks can be replaced with any New York strip loin, bone-in rib-eye, T-bone, or tenderloin steaks.

This recipe is one of my favorite dinners to make on a camping trip: I bring along all the ingredients except for the mushrooms. If I am lucky enough to find them, dinner becomes a feast.

SERVES 4 TO 6

4½ cups sliced fresh porcini mushrooms or 3 ounces dried porcini

2 tablespoons ghee (see page 24), plus more for brushing on the steaks

2 tablespoons finely chopped shallots

1 teaspoon finely chopped fresh rosemary

⅓ cup white wine for fresh mushrooms, ¼ cup plus 3 tablespoons if using dried mushrooms

1 teaspoon lemon juice

1 tablespoon unsalted butter

Flaky sea salt and freshly ground pepper

4 rib-eye bison steaks (see headnote)

2 tablespoons extra-virgin olive oil

If using dried mushrooms, soak them in 2 cups warm water for 15 minutes. Carefully remove the mushrooms and reserve 1 tablespoon of the soaking liquid. If the mushrooms are gritty, pour the soaking liquid through a coffee filter to remove the grit.

Heat the ghee over high heat in a large skillet. Add the mushrooms and sear them undisturbed on one side until browned, about 8 minutes. Add the shallots and rosemary and sauté, stirring, for about 2 more minutes, until the liquid from the mushrooms has evaporated.

Add the white wine and lemon juice. If using dried mushrooms, add the reserved soaking liquid. Cook over high heat until the liquid reduces by one-third. Turn off the heat and swirl in the butter. Add salt and pepper to taste. Set aside and keep warm.

Brush the steaks with some ghee and sprinkle with ½ teaspoon salt and ¼ teaspoon pepper. Grill the steaks or sear them in a cast-iron pan over high heat to an internal temperature of 110°F to 115°F, about 5 minutes per side, depending on the thickness of the steak. Let the meat rest on a platter for 10 minutes before slicing.

Spread the mushroom sauce over the steaks. Drizzle the finished dish with olive oil before serving.

TROUT AMANDINE

Trout is a very healthy fish that is high in omega-3 fatty acids. There is nothing better than catching your own fish and cooking it yourself, but this recipe will of course work with farmed trout you buy in the store, too. To make sure your fish is fresh, press down on the flesh—if it bounces back, it's fresh; if it leaves a dent, it's not.

I like to cook trout whole until crisp, but fillets will work, too. If you're using a whole fish, deboning it prior to cooking will make for an easier dining experience. You can serve it with a side of jasmine rice and a delicate vegetable such as sautéed spinach or asparagus.

SERVES 4

Flaky sea salt and freshly ground black pepper

2 whole trout, cleaned and deboned, or 4 trout fillets

1 large pasture-raised egg

¼ cup half-and-half (ideally raw or nonhomogenized grass-fed)

½ cup home-milled soft white wheat flour (see page 224) or organic whole wheat pastry flour (see Resources, page 264)

¼ cup extra-virgin olive oil

4 tablespoons (½ stick) unsalted butter

1 cup coarsely chopped almonds

3 tablespoons lemon juice

1 tablespoon chopped fresh tarragon, thyme, parsley, or basil

Lemon wedges, for serving

Sprinkle salt and pepper in the cavity of each trout. If using fillets, season them with salt and pepper.

In a shallow dish, beat the egg and whisk in the half-and-half. Put the flour in another shallow dish. Dip the trout into the egg mixture and then the flour. Shake off the excess flour and set the fish aside on a large plate.

Heat the oil in a large skillet over medium-high heat. Add the fish and cook until light brown and flaky on both sides, 6 to 8 minutes per side, depending on the thickness. Transfer the fish to a plate and cover to keep warm.

Return the pan to the heat and melt the butter. Add the almonds and sauté until golden brown. Remove from the heat and add the lemon juice and herbs. Spoon the almonds and butter sauce over the fish and serve with lemon wedges on the side.

CURED TROUT

Making this dish is similar to making ceviche: The trout is "cooked" by the acid in the citrus juice. The typical South American ceviche usually uses spices such as aji or chili peppers to give it a punch of flavor. This cured trout recipe uses only dill, onion, and salt to flavor the dish. The fish cures in the refrigerator for at least two days, creating a silky texture and a smooth taste. This recipe also works well with wild salmon or any other fatty freshwater fish.

SERVES 6

1½ pounds trout fillets, skinned
⅓ cup extra-virgin olive oil, plus 1 tablespoon for coating the baking dish
Juice of 4 lemons
4 whole dill branches
1 large red or white onion, sliced very thinly
Fine sea salt and freshly ground black pepper
Fresh bread, for serving

Chill the trout in the freezer for 30 minutes.

Using a very sharp knife and starting at the tail end, cut diagonal slices as thin as possible.

Coat the bottom of a 6-by-10-inch rectangular glass container or nonreactive baking dish with 1 tablespoon olive oil and sprinkle in 1 tablespoon of the lemon juice.

Layer the baking dish with a third of the trout slices and top them with a third each of the dill, onion, remaining lemon juice, and olive oil, and a pinch of salt and pepper. Repeat two more times to create three layers. Cover with a lid or plastic wrap and refrigerate.

Although the fish has lost its rawness and is ready to eat after about 1 hour, for optimum flavor and texture, let it cure in the refrigerator for at least 2 days.

Serve it with some of the onions and dill and some fresh bread. Cured fish will keep in the refrigerator for up to 1 week.

TROUT JERKY

Any kind of homemade jerky makes a great snack for a hike or a camping trip, as it is nonperishable and provides a good dose of protein. But this trout jerky is the caviar of all jerkies. Made from freshly caught river trout, it is both sweet and salty, and has just the right chewy texture and flavor. The recipe can be made in either a dehydrator or the oven, using low heat.

SERVES 4

One 13-ounce trout fillet, skinned

¼ cup soy sauce

1 teaspoon raw honey

1 garlic clove, crushed

1 tablespoon lemon juice

1 teaspoon freshly ground black pepper

Extra-virgin olive oil, for the oven rack

SPECIAL EQUIPMENT
Dehydrator (optional)

Cut the fish into 1-by-6-inch strips. Make sure the slices are even so they dry at the same rate. Place in a wide shallow bowl.

Combine the soy sauce, honey, garlic, lemon juice, and pepper in a small bowl. Pour the mixture over the fish slices, cover, and let marinate for 4 hours in the refrigerator. Drain and discard the liquid.

To use a dehydrator, lay the fish slices flat on the dehydrator trays. Don't let the fish slices touch. Dry at 145°F to 155°F. The jerky is done when the trout is dry and chewy but not crunchy; start checking for doneness after about 4 hours. Once the strips are cooled, store them in airtight containers or vacuum seal them. They will keep for 2 to 3 months in the refrigerator.

To use the oven, preheat the oven to the lowest possible setting. Wipe an oven rack with olive oil and place the marinated fish directly on the rack. Set a cookie sheet underneath to catch the drippings. Flip the pieces after about 2 hours. The drying time depends on the thickness of the fish slices; check for doneness after about 3 hours. The jerky is ready when there are no moist spots left.

PHEASANT CONFIT

When fall arrives, hunting season begins and game birds like wild pheasant become readily available. Pheasant does not have the same amount of fat as other birds, so it can dry out very quickly, which makes it a good candidate for confit—one of the oldest known methods for preserving meat. To make confit, meat is submerged in fat and cooked very slowly at a low temperature. This dish takes some planning: the pheasant needs to marinate overnight before cooking for 9 hours.

This recipe is an adaptation of classic French duck confit and uses extra duck fat for gentle poaching. It will keep in the refrigerator for two weeks, which makes it a good option for a last-minute meal. To turn it into a main dish, serve it with Crispy Roasted Potatoes (page 95).

SERVES 4

2 tablespoons coarse salt

½ teaspoon freshly ground black pepper

4 pheasant legs

6 garlic cloves, crushed

4 whole thyme branches

4 whole rosemary branches

⅔ cup duck fat (if you don't have duck fat, you can use olive oil instead)

Combine the salt and pepper in a small bowl. Rub both sides of the pheasant legs with the mixture and place them in a large glass container or nonreactive baking dish. Tuck some of the garlic, thyme, and rosemary under the legs and place some on top. Cover with a lid or plastic wrap and refrigerate overnight.

In the morning, brush the rub off the pheasant. Reserve the garlic, thyme, and rosemary.

Preheat the oven to 200°F.

Melt the duck fat in a small sauté pan. Spread the reserved garlic, thyme, and rosemary over the bottom of a Dutch oven. Place the pheasant on top and pour the duck fat over it.

Roast until the meat is very tender and pulls away from the bone, about 9 hours.

Store the pheasant in the fat it cooked in. It will keep in the refrigerator for a couple of weeks.

When ready to serve, scrape away the excess fat, add 1 tablespoon of this fat to a sauté pan, and fry the legs skin side down over medium heat until crisp and the meat is heated through, about 6 minutes.

PINE NUT COOKIES

The best time to forage for pinecones is in the fall. The actual pine nut (*pignoli* in Italian) is located within the scales of the cone. Birds and squirrels eat these nuts as soon as the scales dry and open; to get there ahead of the animals, you'll have to collect closed pinecones and store them in a warm place until they open. Then you can pick the nut from between the scales. The nut is surrounded by a shell, which is soft and thin and can be cracked between your fingers or with the light tap of a small hammer. It's a labor-intensive process, which explains the retail price of pine nuts.

Pine nuts can be used as an accent in many dishes, from salads to pasta; in chocolate bars; and, as in this recipe, in cookies. To get the full flavor of these cookies, use foraged or high-grade pine nuts and homemade almond paste. Pine nuts turn rancid quickly, so smell them before buying them in bulk from a store.

MAKES ABOUT 18 COOKIES

1 cup raw almonds

⅓ cup plus ¼ cup organic cane sugar

1 tablespoon raw honey

1 teaspoon almond extract

1 teaspoon vanilla extract

2 large pasture-raised egg whites

⅓ cup home-milled soft white wheat flour (see page 224) or organic whole wheat pastry flour (see Resources, page 264)

¼ cup plus ⅔ cup pine nuts (see Resources, page 264)

¼ teaspoon fine sea salt

Bring a small saucepan of water to a boil and blanch the almonds for 1 minute. Rinse them with cold water. Rub the skins off with your fingers; discard the skins.

Place the almonds in a food processor and grind into a powder. Add ⅓ cup of the sugar, the honey, and almond extract and blend into fine crumbs. Add the remaining ¼ cup sugar and the vanilla and pulse. Add the egg whites and pulse to combine. Add the flour, ¼ cup pine nuts, and salt; mix just until the dough comes together. The dough will be very wet and sticky. Refrigerate it for 1 hour.

Preheat the oven to 350°F. Line a baking sheet with parchment paper.

Scoop out small balls of dough, about 1½ tablespoons each, and place them 2 inches apart on the prepared baking sheet. Flatten each slightly with a spatula.

Sprinkle the remaining ⅔ cup pine nuts on the cookies.

Bake until the cookies begin to turn golden brown, 18 to 20 minutes. Transfer to a wire rack and let them cool completely. Store them in an airtight container for up to 7 days.

WILD BERRY FOOL

What were the English thinking when, in the sixteenth century, they came up with the name of this dessert? Traditionally, a fool is made by folding stewed or canned fruit into a sweet custard or whipping cream. This dessert becomes lighter when you use fresh fruit instead. The foraged berries are so vibrant with concentrated flavor that you can skip the stewing process and fold them directly into the whipped cream.

MAKES 4 SERVINGS

1 cup heavy whipping cream (ideally raw or nonhomogenized grass-fed)

1 tablespoon organic cane sugar

½ teaspoon vanilla extract

1 pound wild berries (thimbleberries, blackberries, and raspberries work great because they smash up easily)

Pour the whipping cream, sugar, and vanilla into a large bowl and beat with a whisk or an electric mixer until the cream reaches soft peaks. Spoon it into a serving bowl.

In a medium bowl, smash the berries with the back of a fork and fold into the cream. Serve immediately or cover and chill for up to 2 hours.

MOUNTAIN BERRY MARMALADE

This marmalade is made from a mixture of wild harvested berries and serviceberries. Serviceberries (also known as sugar plums) are high in pectin, which makes them a powerful gelling agent. Using serviceberries allows you to get a great marmalade texture without additional sugar or even pectin powder.

There is a large serviceberry tree in our backyard, and we are not the only ones who enjoy its fruits. The tree is also a favorite local hangout for bears. We love watching them from the safety of our house, as they sit up in the branches stuffing themselves. If you do not have access to serviceberries, you can use boiled-down apples as your gelling agent (see page 108).

This recipe makes about 1 cup of marmalade. You can increase quantities and preserve your marmalade. If you are not familiar with sterilizing jars and preparing a canning bath, check out the Resources (page 264).

MAKES ABOUT 1 CUP

1 cup serviceberries

1 cup thimbleberries

1 cup raspberries

¼ cup raw honey, or more to taste

1 tablespoon lemon juice

Combine the berries in a small pot with 1 tablespoon water to avoid burning. Add the honey and lemon juice. Cook for about 10 minutes over high heat while mixing the fruit and mashing it with the back of a fork.

To test if the marmalade is done, drop a spoonful onto a plate. As it cools, if the marmalade stays in place when you tip the plate, it's ready. If it is too thin, boil it down for a little while longer and check it again.

Pour the marmalade into a jar and let it cool down. Secure the lid and refrigerate; it will keep for about 2 weeks.

FRUIT ROLLS

A perennial hiking snack food, fruit rolls are thin layers of pureed fruit that have been dried in a dehydrator or even an oven set at its lowest temperature. Commercial fruit rolls often include unhealthy ingredients. This homemade version uses just three all-natural ingredients: fruit, honey, and lemon juice.

Any berry works great for this recipe. You can also try mangos, apples, plums, peaches, and grapes. Try mixing bananas or dates in with the fruit if it is not sweet enough.

SERVES 4

1 quart wild berries
1 tablespoon raw honey
1 tablespoon lemon juice

SPECIAL EQUIPMENT
Dehydrator (optional)

Place the fruit in a blender with the honey and lemon juice. Puree until smooth.

If using a dehydrator, place a sheet of parchment paper on one of the dehydrator trays. Evenly spread a thin layer of the fruit mixture on the sheet and set the temperature to 140°F.

If using an oven, set the temperature to the lowest setting and spread the fruit puree onto a parchment paper–lined baking sheet.

The fruit rolls should be ready after 5 to 6 hours if using a dehydrator and after about 3 hours if using the oven. They should not be sticky and should easily peel away from the parchment. Gently lift the fruit from the corner and peel it off.

Using a knife or scissors, cut the hardened mixture into 1-inch-wide strips and roll them up. Store in an airtight container. Fruit rolls will keep for up to 1 month at room temperature. To store for up to 1 year, place individual tightly wrapped rolls in the freezer.

WILD BERRY CHOCOLATE BARS

This chocolate treat is actually good for you because cacao is rich in natural antioxidant compounds and has many health benefits.

The process is incredibly easy: you simply melt cacao butter (which is the cold-pressed oil of the cacao bean) and coconut oil, combine them with the rest of the ingredients, pour the mixture into chocolate molds, and freeze it.

While you can change the kind of nuts and dried fruit you use in your chocolate bars, the basic ingredients stay the same. I use dehydrated thimbleberries in these bars, but you could substitute other dried wild berries.

Most of the ingredients should be available at your local health food store; you can also order them online. To find chocolate molds, see Resources (page 264).

MAKES TWO 8-OUNCE CHOCOLATE BARS

3 tablespoons cacao butter (see Resources, page 264)

2 tablespoons coconut oil

¼ cup plus 2 tablespoons ground raw cacao (see Resources, page 264)

2 tablespoons carob powder

2 teaspoons maple sugar or 1½ teaspoons maple syrup

2 tablespoons chopped almonds

1 tablespoon dried wild berries

Dash of vanilla extract

Pinch of fine sea salt

SPECIAL EQUIPMENT
Chocolate molds

Pour an inch of water into a large saucepan and bring to a simmer over high heat, then reduce the heat to low.

Put the cacao butter and coconut oil in a metal mixing bowl (slightly wider than the saucepan) and set it on top of the saucepan, making sure it does not touch the water. When the mixture is melted, remove the bowl from the heat.

In a small bowl, combine the ground cacao, carob powder, maple sugar, almonds, dried berries, vanilla, and salt. Add the melted cacao butter and coconut oil and mix everything together with a spoon.

Pour the mixture into the chocolate molds. If you don't have chocolate molds, you can use ice cube trays, bowls, or pans instead. Let the mixture cool to room temperature and place the molds in the freezer to set for at least 2 hours. Remove the chocolate from the molds and wrap it in parchment paper. This chocolate has a very low melting point, so it will get soft at room temperature. The refrigerator is not an ideal environment for storing chocolate because cacao butter easily absorbs the flavor of other food, so store the chocolate in the freezer for up to 6 months or eat it all at once.

RED CLOVER
ICED TEA

Red clover—rich in calcium, magnesium, niacin, and vitamin C—can be found in fields, open forests, and lawns across North America and Europe. Be careful when harvesting; you don't want to forage where pesticides may have been sprayed.

Red clover's flower season is between April and October, but you can easily dry the flowers and enjoy this healthy tea any time of year. To dry the flowers, remove the stems and spread the blossoms out on trays. Dry them away from direct sunlight as the sun will brown the flowers. After 48 hours, the blossoms should feel completely dry.

You can also dry red clover blossoms in a dehydrator: Set the temperature to 120°F. Check them after a couple of hours to see if they are dry. Store the dried flowers in an airtight container in a cool, dry, and dark place.

If you don't have access to red clover blossoms you can buy them online (see Resources, page 264).

This tea is not recommended for pregnant women or young children, or for anyone taking blood-thinning medication.

MAKES 1 QUART

1 cup fresh or dried red clover blossoms
3 tablespoons raw honey
Juice of 1 lemon

Fill a teakettle with 1 quart water, add the red clover blossoms, and bring to a boil.

Let the water boil for 5 minutes, then turn off the heat. Add the honey, stir, and let the tea steep for 2 hours.

Strain the tea through a fine-mesh sieve, discarding the flowers. Add the lemon juice, stir, and refrigerate the tea to chill it before serving.

BY
THE
FIRE

TUSCAN-GRILLED PIZZA 172

CHEESE FONDUE 179

RACLETTE 183

BRATWURST 184

SMOKED WILD SALMON 188

SMOKED WILD SALMON MOUSSE 193

ROSEMARY-FLAVORED POPCORN 194

CAMPFIRE WAFFLES 196

APPLES COOKED IN HOT COALS 200

APPLE CAKE 202

CHOCOLATE FONDUE 205

GLÜHWEIN 206

PINE NEEDLE TEA 210

Throw a pot over those open flames and soon even more options abound.

—JULIA CHILD

Once humans knew how to make fire, they started cooking food they found in nature, and this simple act accelerated human evolution. So fire is at the core of our being. Whether I cook in my kitchen, outdoors on a Tuscan grill, or in the wild on a campfire, I always cook with my family and friends in mind. Often they're beside me, helping me chop, stir, or grill or collecting kindling and building the fire pit.

The fear of starting a forest fire can spoil any outdoor meal, so safety is important before you begin. If it's windy, you should build your fire in a place that is shielded; if it's dry, look for a spot near the water. If your site is dense with trees and brush, clear a large area around the pit. But if this damages the landscape—and I prefer to leave no trace at all—be as gentle as possible. In a rocky area, a large flat stone is an excellent base for a fire; I get my kids to stack lots of rocks around the fire pit. But my favorite place to build a fire is an open space by the side of a stream. The sound of the water rushing by, as I watch the kids rolling up their pants to play, makes it the perfect spot.

I let the fire burn down and then I cook everything from homemade bratwurst (see page 184) and foraged mushrooms to Pine Needle Tea (page 210) over the glowing embers. I prefer to make things that we have gathered or hunted, rather than lug too many supplies into the forest, but I have been known to carry cast-iron pans and even a waffle iron (see page 196) just to create the perfect outdoor meal. The thrill of cooking outdoors is the dream of going back to the wild, so any reminders of the modern world, like plastic utensils, can taint the experience.

You don't have to live in the mountains or near the woods to set up camp and cook outdoors. America has many national and state forests with campgrounds, even near big cities, where you can have this experience. You can also evoke the feeling of a campfire by building an outdoor fire pit at home and using a Tuscan grill (see page 176). Use it to make grilled pizza (see page 172), and gather around the fire for Cheese Fondue (page 179) and Chocolate Fondue (page 205).

See Resources (page 264) for information on locating your nearest park or campground.

TUSCAN-GRILLED PIZZA

Flatbread is traditionally cooked on hot stones over an open fire. A Tuscan grill (see page 176) is a great accessory to use with this method. If you don't have a Tuscan grill, place bricks on either side of the fire to support a grill rack. Because the heat comes only from below, you must first grill the dough on one side and then add the toppings on the toasted side. This is perfect party fare; lay out a buffet of toppings, and guests can build their own flatbread pizzas.

SERVES 5

DOUGH

2¾ cups home-milled farro flour (see page 224) or 2½ cups organic spelt flour (see Resources, page 264), plus more for forming the dough

½ cup home-milled soft white wheat flour (see page 224) or organic whole wheat pastry flour (see Resources, page 264)

1 tablespoon extra-virgin olive oil, plus more for brushing the dough

1½ teaspoons fine sea salt

½ teaspoon active dry yeast

ASSORTED TOPPINGS

Fresh mozzarella

Fresh vegetables, such as mushrooms, tomatoes, and eggplant

Tomato sauce

Fresh basil

SPECIAL EQUIPMENT

Tuscan grill

continued

Combine the flours and 1¼ cups water in a large bowl and let soak overnight to soften the grains.

In the morning, add the olive oil, salt, and yeast. Knead everything together in the bowl, incorporating some extra flour if needed to create a smooth dough, 5 to 7 minutes. Form it into a ball.

Cover the dough with a kitchen towel and let it rise for 1½ hours.

If cooking in the fireplace or outdoors, build a fire (see page 176). As the flames in the fire subside, place the Tuscan grill directly above the fire.

Meanwhile, turn the dough out onto a floured surface. Divide it into four equal pieces and place them on a large plate covered with a towel. Stretch the first piece into a 12-inch round. Hold the dough in your hands and let gravity help you stretch it, or stretch it on a clean board or a plate. If the dough is sticky, coat it with additional flour to make it easier to work with.

Once the wood in the fire has burned down to hot embers, brush both sides of the flattened dough with olive oil and place it directly on the grill. When one side of the dough is toasted, remove it from the fireplace and add cheese plus any other toppings you choose on the toasted side. Repeat with the other dough pieces.

Once the underside of the pizza is nicely charred and all the cheese is melted, about 5 minutes, the pizza is ready. Repeat with the remaining dough.

To bake the pizzas in a conventional oven, set a pizza stone on the middle rack and preheat to 550°F. Ten minutes before placing the pizza in the oven, lower the temperature to 450°F. Add toppings and bake for 15 minutes, until the crust is lightly browned.

CREATING A FIRE FOR OUTDOOR COOKING

To build a good fire for cooking, the first thing you need to do is gather tinder, kindling, and logs. The tinder is what you need to start the fire; it can include dry twigs, leaves, and newspaper. Kindling is dry sticks that are slightly larger than tinder and burn easily. For the logs, the best woods to use for cooking are oak, nut trees, hickory, pecan, or fruit trees. Look for dry wood without any odor.

Safety is important, so find the right spot for your fire. If it's windy, you'll want to build it in a shielded area. If the ground is very dry, try to build your fire near a stream, pond, or lake. If the site is dense with trees and brush, clear a large area around the pit, without damaging the landscape. In a rocky area, a large flat stone makes an excellent base for a fire.

Fill the fire pit with tinder, and place kindling on top of it in alternating directions. Start the fire by lighting the tinder. As the kindling catches fire, add larger pieces of dry hardwood on top until you have a robust campfire. Now you need to wait for the flames to die down because the heat over open flames is not consistent and there is a higher chance of burning the outside of your food before the inside is fully cooked. When the fire burns down, place the food directly over the hot coals to take advantage of the direct, intense heat of your smoldering fire.

Depending on the method of cooking, you can also use a Tuscan grill, which is a sturdy cast-iron grate with legs to place over a fire (see Resources, page 264), or you can balance a rack on two rocks, as for Tuscan-Grilled Pizza (page 172), Campfire Waffles (page 196), or Apple Cake (page 202). You can also cook food directly in the coals, as for Apples Cooked in Hot Coals (page 200).

For Cheese Fondue (page 179), Raclette (page 183), or Chocolate Fondue (page 205), it is best to use indirect heat. Indirect heat can be created by placing the food you are cooking farther away from the hot coals, either higher or on the grate slightly to the side, to get a cooler temperature.

CHEESE FONDUE

Fondue is the national dish of my homeland, Switzerland. Each town has its own special fondue cheese mix, which evolves from the local cheese production. If you are experimenting with your own local cheeses, look for hard cheeses with a fat content of 45 percent or more, since these are the best for melting. And the older the cheese, the richer the flavor.

Use a traditional shallow fondue pot or a small ceramic-coated cast-iron pot to cook and serve the fondue. The cheese needs to be constantly heated, even while people are eating it. Traditionally a fondue pot is placed on top of a metal stand (often sold with the fondue pot) that holds the pot over an adjustable flame. But I love cooking and eating fondue fireside, with the open fire keeping the fondue heated. It's a great meal to bring along on a camping trip: pack the shredded cheese and cornstarch together, and pack the white wine, lemon juice, cognac, mustard powder, and baguettes separately.

The crust left at the bottom of the pot is called *la croûte*. Scrape it off and serve it to your guests. It is considered a delicacy.

SERVES 8

FONDUE
1 garlic clove, cut in half

2 pounds shredded cheese (my favorite combinations are 1 pound Gruyère and 1 pound Comté, and 11 ounces Gruyère, 11 ounces Appenzeller, and 10 ounces Emmentaler)

3 tablespoons cornstarch

2⅓ cups dry white wine, such as Sauvignon Blanc

2 tablespoons lemon juice

1 tablespoon cognac (optional; you can also use kirsch or Poire William)

1 tablespoon mustard powder

FOR DIPPING
2 baguettes, such as a rustic sourdough or a ciabatta, cut into bite-sized cubes

SPECIAL EQUIPMENT
Fondue pot

Build a fire (see page 176 for instructions).

Rub the cut garlic clove all over the inside of the fondue pot.

If the cheese and cornstarch are not already together in a container for transport, combine them in a large bowl.

continued

CHEESE FONDUE *continued*

Pour the wine and lemon juice into the fondue pot. Place a flat rock or a Tuscan grill (see Resources, page 264) a couple of inches away from the flames of your fire to use indirect heat, set the pot on top of the rock or grill, and bring to a gentle simmer.

Gradually add the cheeses and cornstarch to the simmering liquid. Stir continuously to make sure the cheese melts gradually. After about 10 minutes, when the mixture thickens and has a smooth consistency, stir in the cognac and mustard.

Keep the fondue close to the fire while eating it to keep the cheese from solidifying. Serve with bread cubes for dipping.

Cover leftover fondue and keep it in a cool place. Simply reheat the fondue until the cheese melts and returns to its creamy texture. Leftover fondue can be kept for up to 1 week in the refrigerator.

RACLETTE

For raclette, a traditional Swiss dish, a wheel of cheese is melted, and the melted part is scraped off and eaten with boiled potatoes, charcuterie, and pickles. There are two types of raclette melting machines: an electric tabletop device that melts individual portions of cheese and another that holds a quarter of a wheel and melts the cheese under a heat lamp. But I prefer to melt raclette and eat it around an open fire, which is the same way Swiss cowherds have eaten it for centuries.

SERVES 4

12 small new potatoes, unpeeled
2 pounds raclette
Assorted dry cured meats, such as Bündnerfleisch and prosciutto, cut into thin slices
Cornichons and pickled onions

If your cheese has been refrigerated, remove it from the refrigerator a couple of hours before cooking. If you will be melting the cheese by the fire, build your fire (see page 176).

About half an hour before you want to heat the raclette, fill a medium pot with water and bring it to a boil. Add the potatoes and cook until fork-tender, about 20 minutes. Keep warm.

Assemble a charcuterie platter, including the dry-cured meats, cornichons, and pickled onions.

When the flames have died down, place the cheese wheel close to the fire, either on a stand that holds the cheese or on a clean stone, with the cut side facing the fire. When the cheese begins to melt, place a few potatoes on the plates and use a spatula to spread the cheese over the potatoes.

If using a raclette grill, each person takes a slice of cheese, places it on the individual pans, slides it under the grill, and lets it melt until bubbly, which takes about 2 minutes. Place the potatoes on the plate and spread the cheese over the potatoes.

BRATWURST

Bratwurst is a German sausage made from a mixture of finely ground pork and veal. Each region in Germany has its own version. Bratwurst is often sold by street vendors in Germany, Austria, and Switzerland, but this street food can also make a great lunch or dinner at home when you serve it with a side of crusty rustic bread, Dijon mustard, and a salad.

When you make your own sausages, you control what goes into them. This recipe calls for 100-percent grass-fed meat and sea salt, and no additives or preservatives.

A wide selection of sausage stuffers and meat grinders is available online or in kitchen supply stores in every price range (see Resources, page 264). If you own a stand mixer, you can get a food grinder attachment and a sausage stuffer kit. It's an economical solution and doesn't take up much storage space. If you don't have a sausage stuffer, shape the meat into patties and fry them in a pan.

MAKES TWELVE 4-INCH SAUSAGES

Hog casings, 32 mm to 35 mm (optional; see Resources, page 264)

2 pounds grass-fed pork butt with fat (about ¾ pound fat)

1 pound grass-fed veal shoulder

1 tablespoon fine sea salt, plus more to taste

½ teaspoon freshly ground black pepper, plus more to taste

½ teaspoon ground mace

½ teaspoon grated lemon zest

½ teaspoon ground marjoram

Ghee (see page 24), if frying sausage patties or links in a pan

SPECIAL EQUIPMENT
Meat grinder

Sausage stuffer

To use the hog casings, soak them in a bowl filled with tepid water for 1 hour. Rinse well with cool water and place in a sieve to drain.

Cut the pork and veal into 1-inch pieces. Chill the meat and the grinder or blade in the freezer for 30 minutes. This is an important step; otherwise, the heat from the blade may cause the meat to smear, creating a pulpy texture in the finished sausage. Using the finest grind on your machine, grind the meat mixture into a large bowl. Bratwurst is a very finely ground sausage, so send the meat through the grinder twice. (If you don't have a meat grinder, have your butcher freshly grind the meat for you.)

continued

BRATWURST *continued*

Add the salt, pepper, mace, lemon zest, and marjoram. Mix by hand until the meat binds together and the mixture is very sticky.

You can test the flavor by frying a small patty in a sauté pan. Taste and adjust the seasoning if needed.

To form the sausage into links, thread a hog casing over the sausage stuffer. Tie a knot at the end of the casing. Hold the casing as you feed the meat through the stuffer. Once you have stuffed the casing with sausage, tie a knot at the other end. Pinch and twist the sausage into about 4-inch links by turning each section 4 times in opposite directions, creating 4 to 5 sausages per casing. Repeat with the remaining filling and casings. To form into individual sausages, cut through each of the twisted casing and tie knots on both ends of the sausage, gently pushing in the stuffing to give you enough room to tie a knot. If you are not using casings, form the meat mixture into patties as if making hamburgers. You can refrigerate the sausages or patties for up to 3 days or freeze them for 1 month.

If cooking indoors, heat a skillet over medium-low heat. Coat the pan with ghee and fry the sausages/patties until brown and cooked through, about 5 minutes on each side.

If cooking the bratwurst outdoors, build a fire (see page 176). You can cook the individual sausages on a stick or in a pan, placing the pan directly on the hot coals or on a grate set over the flames. Keep turning the sausage to ensure that it cooks evenly.

SMOKED WILD SALMON

I love being able to catch my own fish, but sadly, there are no wild salmon in the rivers of Colorado. So when salmon is in season, between June and September, I get a whole fresh fish from my local market. Wild king salmon is the fattiest of the salmon family, which gives it a great texture and flavor. It's a healthy choice, too, because of its high levels of omega-3 fatty acids.

There are two ways to make this recipe. You can smoke the salmon using alder chips over an open fire, which will give it a great rich and earthy flavor, or you can use alder chips to smoke the fish indoors on your stovetop.

SERVES 4

1½ pounds wild salmon fillet, bones removed
¼ cup coarse sea salt
¼ cup packed light brown sugar
1 tablespoon grated lemon zest

SPECIAL EQUIPMENT
Handful of alder chips

Place a large piece of foil on the counter and top with an equally large piece of parchment paper. Place the salmon on top of the parchment and season both sides with the salt, sugar, and lemon zest. Wrap tightly, place on a plate, and put something heavy on top to weigh it down (I usually use a cast-iron skillet). Refrigerate for about 8 hours.

Place the alder chips in a bowl and cover with water for 30 minutes.

Drain the water and place the alder chips in the bottom of a large wok with a wire rack set inside. Unwrap the salmon and place it skin side down on the rack. Cover with a lid or a large sheet of foil. Crimp the foil along the edge of the pan to seal it tightly.

To smoke the salmon outdoors, build a fire (see page 176). Place the wok to the side of the fire. Using the indirect heat of the fire will prevent it from overcooking. Let it smoke until the salmon is firm to the touch and a glaze forms on the surface, about 40 minutes. Check periodically on the smoke inside the wok by removing the cover or picking up one edge of the foil. Rotate the wok periodically so the salmon cooks evenly. Place the pan closer to the fire if the smoke disappears.

To smoke the salmon on your stove, temporarily disable your smoke detector. Heat the wok with the salmon over high heat. Once it starts to produce a good amount of smoke, lower the heat to medium.

Let the salmon rest, covered in the wok, for 5 minutes before serving.

SMOKED WILD SALMON MOUSSE

Salmon mousse is an easy way to use leftover smoked salmon. The smoked salmon adds an unusual and rich taste to the ricotta cheese and, when blended together, they form a smooth paste that spreads nicely over a piece of crusty bread. It can be served as a canapé, an appetizer, or an elegant snack.

MAKES ABOUT 1 CUP

1 cup ricotta cheese (see page 27)

7 ounces smoked salmon (see page 188), bones removed

1 tablespoon chopped fresh chives

1 teaspoon flaky sea salt

Crusty bread, for serving

Place the ricotta and salmon in a blender and blend for a few seconds, until the mixture has the consistency of a mousse.

Place the mousse in a small bowl and stir in the chives and salt.

Serve immediately or store in a closed container in the refrigerator for up to 1 week.

ROSEMARY-FLAVORED POPCORN

Popping corn over an open fire is an edible adventure, as it may take a couple of tries to get the perfect batch. You have to use all your senses—listening for the sound of popping kernels, sniffing for any hint of scorched corn—and guess when the last few are done, while you shake the container regularly to make sure that the popped corn doesn't burn (see Resources, page 264, for a camping edition popcorn popper). Of course, you can use the same recipe to make popcorn indoors on your stove.

SERVES 4

4 tablespoons (½ stick) butter

3 fresh rosemary sprigs

⅔ cup popcorn kernels

2 tablespoons truffle oil

¾ teaspoon flaky sea salt

SPECIAL EQUIPMENT
Campfire popcorn popper (optional)

If cooking outdoors, build a fire (see page 176).

Place the butter and rosemary sprigs in a small pan. Heat over low flames (or, if indoors, on the stove over low heat) for 10 minutes, until the butter is melted. Remove from the heat and let the butter cool to room temperature. Remove and discard the rosemary sprigs.

Put the popcorn kernels in a medium bowl and mix in the melted butter. Pour the buttered popcorn into the popcorn popper and close the lid. Hold the popper directly over the fire. Once the popcorn starts to pop, hold it farther away from the fire. Shake the popper once in a while so the kernels and butter don't burn.

To make the popcorn on the stove, put the kernels in a large pot, cover it with a lid, and set over medium-high heat. Once you hear the popcorn starting to pop, reduce the heat to low. Shake the pot once in a while so the kernels don't burn.

You'll know the popcorn is ready when you stop hearing the pop of the kernels. Transfer the popcorn to a large bowl, drizzle with the truffle oil, toss well, and season with the salt.

CAMPFIRE WAFFLES

Few things in life are more enjoyable to me than getting up with the sun, rekindling a campfire, and cooking breakfast. I'm the kind of person who brings a waffle iron when camping because I think waffles taste best in the wild, cooked over an open fire and served with cream and foraged berries. Of course, these waffles can also be made at home, over a Tuscan grill or indoors with a traditional waffle maker.

Buttermilk not only gives a nice flavor to the waffles but also softens and enriches the grains (see Note, page 223). Look for grass-fed buttermilk at your local health food store, and try to avoid buttermilk with added gums or stabilizers.

MAKES 12 WAFFLES

1 cup buttermilk

1½ cups home-milled soft white wheat flour (see page 224) or organic whole wheat pastry flour (see Resources, page 264)

½ cup oat flour

1 teaspoon baking powder

½ teaspoon baking soda

½ teaspoon fine sea salt

¾ cup milk (ideally raw or nonhomogenized grass-fed)

3 tablespoons maple syrup

2 large pasture-raised egg yolks, lightly beaten

4 tablespoons (½ stick) butter, melted, plus more for serving (optional)

1 teaspoon vanilla extract

3 large pasture-raised egg whites, beaten until stiff

Ghee (see page 24), for greasing the waffle iron

Berries (optional)

Whipped Cream (recipe follows; optional)

Maple syrup (optional)

SPECIAL EQUIPMENT
Campfire or electric waffle iron (see Resources, page 264)

continued

Combine the buttermilk and the flours in a large bowl. Cover and let the mixture sit overnight at room temperature.

The next morning, build a fire if cooking outdoors (see page 176). Combine the baking powder, baking soda, and salt in a small bowl. Add to the batter and mix well.

Combine the milk, maple syrup, egg yolks, melted butter, and vanilla in a medium bowl and add to the batter. Do not overmix.

Gently fold the beaten egg whites into the batter.

Once the flames die down, place the waffle iron on a Tuscan grill (see page 176) or balance a grate on two rocks and set it over the hot coals. After a couple of minutes, turn the waffle iron over to heat the other side.

When the iron is very hot, grease it well with ghee and pour in the batter; do not overfill. Cook for 2 minutes, flip over, and cook for another 2 minutes. Carefully lift—if there is a bit of resistance, cook for another 30 seconds and check again until the waffles are golden brown. Butter the iron well each time before adding more batter. Serve topped with berries and whipped cream or butter and maple syrup.

Use an electric waffle maker to cook the waffles at home. To get them as crispy as those cooked over an open flame, preheat your oven to 250°F. Place cooked waffles directly on the oven rack for 7 minutes, turn them over, and bake for another 7 minutes.

WHIPPED CREAM

MAKES 1 CUP

1 cup heavy whipping cream (ideally raw or nonhomogenized grass-fed)
1 tablespoon light brown sugar
½ teaspoon vanilla extract

Pour the cream, sugar, and vanilla into a large bowl and beat with a whisk or an electric mixer until soft peaks form.

APPLES COOKED
IN HOT COALS

Once your campfire dies down and you're left with glowing embers, you have the perfect conditions for cooking apples. The apples get stuffed with raisins and nuts, spiced with cinnamon, and sweetened with honey. Then you wrap them in foil and place them directly on the hot coals. The cooked apples come out soft and infused with the sweetness of the plumped raisins and the aroma of cinnamon. Serve with the cooking juices spooned over the top.

SERVES 4

4 large apples, such as Honeycrisp, Pink Lady, or Crispin

½ cup raisins

½ cup chopped walnuts

¼ cup plus 1 tablespoon raw honey

4 cinnamon sticks or 1 tablespoon ground cinnamon

4 teaspoons unsalted butter

Build a fire (see page 176) and let it burn down to hot embers.

Place each apple on a large square of parchment paper. Using a paring knife, cut off the top part of the apple with the stem and reserve the tops. Push a paring knife through the apple and cut around the core, leaving the bottom ½ inch of the apples intact. With a small spoon, dig out the remaining core. Make the holes about 1 inch wide.

Combine the raisins, walnuts, honey, and ground cinnamon, if using, in a small bowl.

Fill each apple cavity with the nut mixture. If using the cinnamon sticks, place one in each cavity. Top each apple with 1 teaspoon of the butter.

Set the reserved tops back on the apples and wrap tightly, first with parchment paper, then with foil.

When the coals are red and glowing, they are ready to use. Place the apples directly in the coals and cook for about 25 minutes, rolling the packets from side to side with long-handled tongs every couple of minutes. Remove from the fire and allow the apples to cool for approximately 5 minutes. Unwrap and serve. Eat the apples with a fork and knife.

APPLE CAKE

This cake is a prep-ahead dessert for your next camping trip. You can premix the sugar, flour, baking powder, salt, and walnuts and put them in an airtight container. You'll need to bring the other ingredients separately. When you're ready to cook the cake over an open fire, add the vanilla, egg, apple, and butter to your container and pour everything into a cast-iron pan. Of course, good apple cake can also be made in your oven at home.

SERVES 4

½ cup home-milled soft white wheat flour (see page 224) or organic whole wheat pastry flour (see Resources, page 264)

⅓ cup organic cane sugar

1 teaspoon baking powder

⅛ teaspoon fine sea salt

½ cup chopped walnuts

1 large pasture-raised egg

½ teaspoon vanilla extract

1 cup peeled and chopped Granny Smith apples

1 tablespoon unsalted butter

Build a fire (see page 176) and let it burn down to hot embers. On each side of the fire, arrange a platform of rocks that can support a grate for cooking (you can use an oven or grill rack) 4 to 6 inches above the coals. Set an 8-inch cast-iron skillet with a lid over the hot coals to preheat it.

Combine the flour, sugar, baking powder, salt, and walnuts in a large bowl. (Put them in an airtight container if you're prepping the cake for a camping trip.)

Mix the egg and vanilla in a small bowl and add it to the flour mixture. Fold in the chopped apple.

Remove the hot skillet from the grate, coat it with the butter, and pour in the batter. Cover with a lid.

Use a stick to level the coals. Place the covered skillet back on the rack.

After about 15 minutes, shovel a pile of the hot coals on top of the covered pan. After 10 minutes, using leather gloves and pliers or a lid lifter, brush the coals aside, lift the lid, and watch for hot spots where areas of the cake might be browning too quickly and rotate the pan. After another 10 minutes, lift the lid again and check for doneness: a knife inserted into the center of the cake should come out clean and the top should be nicely browned. Serve warm or at room temperature.

To bake the cake in an oven, preheat the oven to 350°F. Pour the batter into a buttered 10-inch cast-iron skillet or 10-inch round cake pan and bake uncovered. After 30 minutes, check for doneness: a knife inserted into the center of the cake should come out clean and the top should be nicely browned.

CHOCOLATE FONDUE

This recipe uses dark chocolate, which gives the fondue a rich cocoa taste, but if you prefer a sweeter, creamier flavor, use milk chocolate. You can use a fondue pot to melt the chocolate, but a ceramic-coated cast-iron pot will also work. The chocolate needs to stay heated even while you're eating it, so traditionally the fondue pot is placed on top of a metal stand (sold with the pot) set over an adjustable flame. Instead, try cooking and eating the fondue fireside, using the low flames to keep the chocolate warm and melted. Serve with long fondue forks for dipping.

FONDUE
2 cups half-and-half (ideally raw or nonhomogenized grass-fed)

½ pound bittersweet or semisweet chocolate, about 65% cacao, broken into small chunks

1 teaspoon vanilla extract

FOR DIPPING
Biscotti (page 261)

Pretzel sticks

Banana pieces

Apple pieces

Strawberries

Dried apricots

SPECIAL EQUIPMENT
Fondue pot

Skewers

Build a fire (see page 176) and let it burn down to embers. Use a long stick to spread out the coals to lower their heat. On each side of the fire, arrange a platform of rocks that can support a grate for cooking

Pour the half-and-half into a small heatproof pan. Set the pan on the grate and heat the half-and-half over the coals until it comes to a low boil. Remove the grate and place the fondue pot directly on the rock using the indirect heat of the fire. Add the chocolate and vanilla. Let it melt slowly while stirring.

Arrange the food for dipping on a large platter and serve with long fondue forks to dip the fruit or cookies into the hot melted chocolate.

Pour leftover chocolate into a container. Let it cool down, cover, and store in the refrigerator. You can keep leftovers for up to 2 weeks. Remelt to eat.

GLÜHWEIN

Hot spiced wine is a traditional winter drink that can be found in many northern countries under different names like glögg, mulled wine, or bishop's wine. In Switzerland, it is called glühwein, which literally means "glow wine." After a long winter's day spent outdoors, skiing, sledding, snowshoeing, or simply taking a walk, the hot cup of glühwein will indeed thaw your entire body and give you a glow.

MAKES 3 CUPS

8 whole cloves

2 oranges, cut in half

1 bottle of red wine, such as a Cabernet Sauvignon

1 lemon, cut in half

3 cinnamon sticks

2 star anise

¼ cup raw honey

½ cup rum (optional)

If mulling the wine outdoors, build a fire (see page 176). On each side of the fire, arrange a platform of rocks that can support a grate for cooking.

Stick the cloves into the rind of the orange halves.

In a medium pot, combine the oranges, wine, lemon, cinnamon sticks, and star anise. Set the pot on a grate over the hot coals or over medium-high heat on a stove and bring to a boil. Use a stick to move away some of the hot embers or lower the heat on the stove and let the wine simmer for about 20 minutes.

Remove the lemon and orange halves, squeezing the juices into the wine, and discard the cloves and rinds. Add the honey and rum, if using. Strain into a large pitcher and serve hot. Leftovers can be kept covered in the refrigerator for 1 week.

PINE NEEDLE TEA

Hunters, settlers, and indigenous people around the world have made tea from pine needles for centuries and—according to legend—it even has healing powers. One cup of pine needle tea contains up to five times the amount of vitamin C in a lemon, which makes it a potent antioxidant and an immune system booster. It is also reported to have decongestant properties. When you collect the needles for the tea, pick the young, light green ones at the tips of the branches. White pine is a great choice. Avoid Ponderosa, Lodgepole, and Monterey pine tree needles, which are highly toxic. You can recognize white pine by its longer, softer needles.

This tea is not recommended for pregnant women and young children.

MAKES 1 QUART

1 cup ½-inch-long chopped white pine needles, sheaths at base of needles removed

Juice of 1 lemon (optional)

Raw honey (optional)

Fill a teakettle with 1 quart water and bring to a boil over your campfire (see page 176) or the stove.

When the water boils, remove it from the heat and add the pine needles. Let steep for 20 minutes.

Strain the tea, discard the pine needles, and serve hot. Add lemon juice and honey to taste, if you'd like.

THROUGH THE MILL

ILONA'S CRUNCH 220

HOME-MILLED OATMEAL 226

OATMEAL BAKED APPLES 229

BIRCHERMÜESLI 233

ANCIENT GRAIN PANCAKES 237

CORN BREAD 240

HEARTY BREAD 243

SAVORY TART DOUGH 247

SWEET TART DOUGH 249

BREAD PUDDING 250

GIANT CHOCOLATE CHIP COOKIE 253

BANANA BREAD 254

WAFFLE CONES 257

BISCOTTI 261

Daily, our eating turns nature into culture, transforming the body of the world into our bodies and minds.

—MICHAEL POLLAN, *THE OMNIVORE'S DILEMMA*

Being pregnant with my first child made a huge impact on the evolution of my cooking. I'd gone through the stage of making challenging and complicated recipes; I'd become conscious of the value of fresh, locally grown produce and knew the importance of organic and humanely raised livestock. But it wasn't until I read Michael Pollan's *The Omnivore's Dilemma* that I fully understood the consequences of what we put into our bodies. I became acutely aware that everything I ate was also my baby's nutrition, which felt like a huge responsibility, and the more I read, the more concerned I became.

Pollan's lists of artificial ingredients had me obsessed with reading labels. I spent hours in the supermarket, as if it were the library, taking things off the shelf, studying the unpronounceable contents, and putting them back on the shelf. Over the next few months, I arrived at the checkout counter with an ever-diminishing amount of packaged goods in my basket.

I learned how commercial flours are mass-produced—how they are genetically manipulated, sprayed with chemicals, and stripped of their most nutritious elements. Then I researched milling my own grain and bought my first flour mill so I could make baby cereal and teething biscuits. My next challenge was to replace my husband Chad's favorite Grape-Nuts cereal with a healthier version. This mix is called Ilona's Crunch (page 220), and we've been eating it ever since.

The value that is added by milling your own grains is amazing, from cost and flavor to uniqueness and nutritional value. When bought in bulk, home-milled grains are cheaper than store-bought flour. And because each grain is different, you can work with all kinds of flour. Commercial flour is dull compared to the fresh flavor of home-milled flour. I have also learned to soak grains prior to cooking them, a process that makes them easier to digest and improves the absorption of minerals into our systems (see "Soaking Grains," page 218).

The flour mill is my favorite piece of kitchen equipment; I use it to mill grains for bread, baked treats, homemade breakfast cereal, and tarts, and I flake oat groats for Home-Milled Oatmeal (page 226) or Birchermüesli (page 233). Once I incorporated milling into my daily routine, it became an integral part of my kitchen work. Grinding grain is a simple process that takes only a few extra minutes; you'll notice the difference when you use this flour to make Hearty Bread (page 243), Ancient Grain Pancakes (page 237), Corn Bread (page 240), and Waffle Cones (page 257).

I make the majority of our meals, treats, and snacks from scratch. It's a state of mind now, and I could never go back, yet sometimes I wonder if my kids are missing out on some

typical childhood experiences, like eating Oreos or taking trips to Dunkin' Donuts. But when Hendrix comes home from school lamenting the junk-food lunches of some of his classmates, I know that he likes his healthy lunch.

I've always tried to make cooking and eating into a special experience for my kids, and I hope my enthusiasm has rubbed off on them. As soon as Hendrix was old enough, Chad and I involved him in finding and picking fresh food, and cooking is something we do together as a family. By the time Liloo was born, our rituals had become habit, and picking food and cooking at home seems to come naturally to her, as if she has an instinctive connection to how nature will sustain her.

But we also have to realize that nature is under siege as humans cultivate more and more land to support their growing needs. For instance, many more people are gluten intolerant now, and research has found that this exponential rise is linked to the increased use of pesticides, crop stimulants, and genetically modified seeds. It is worth buying organic grain with a non-GMO heritage instead of supermarket products made from flour whose origins are unclear. Bread, cookies, croutons, cereal, crackers, and all other baked goods that are made from scratch with home-milled grains may lead the way to more sustainable living. If we can all teach our children this way of life, one that integrates nature on every level, we can change the perception of food, reduce our "foodprint," and make the planet a healthier place.

To find fresh grains, first try to locate a local grain supplier. If there is no grain supplier or mill in your area, see Resources (page 264).

SOAKING GRAINS

I learned from Sally Fallon, author of *Nourishing Traditions*, how to soak grains prior to cooking them. Soaking helps to neutralize the grains' antinutrients, which makes the grains easier to digest and improves the absorption of minerals. (Antinutrients are components such as phytic acid and enzyme inhibitors that, even in healthy foods, interfere with nutrient absorption.) In most recipes, I add the soaking time for the milled flour. However, I always try to have some soaked grains on hand for making cookies, tart doughs, or bread. Here are some guidelines for soaking grains.

Place the grains in a bowl. Cover with water and stir in 1 tablespoon of acidic solution (apple cider vinegar, lemon juice, or whey). Cover the bowl with a dish towel and let the grains soak for 12 hours, at room temperature, then drain.

To dry the grains using your oven, preheat the oven to the lowest possible setting. Line a baking pan with parchment paper and spread the grains on it. Bake until the grains are completely dry, 6 to 8 hours, depending on the temperature of the oven. To use a dehydrator, dry the grains at 145°F until completely dry, about 12 hours.

Place the grains in sealed containers and store in the refrigerator for up to 6 months or in the freezer for up to 1 year.

ILONA'S CRUNCH

This breakfast cereal is the result of a challenge by my husband to create a healthy alternative to Grape-Nuts, which he used to eat every morning. After much experimenting and adjusting, I finally had him try this recipe. He loved it and named it after me, and now this cereal is our breakfast staple. It uses several whole grains, each with its own health benefits. The combination of the grains and legumes makes it a nutritional superfood; it gets its crunch from being baked with molasses.

Serve with milk and top with fruit, raisins, and nuts, or eat as a trail mix combined with nuts and dried fruit.

MAKES ABOUT 12 SERVINGS

1⅔ cups oat groats

1⅓ cups hard red winter wheat berries, spelt, or farro

⅓ cup amaranth

⅓ cup lentils

⅓ cup barley

⅓ cup buckwheat groats

¼ cup dried corn kernels

2¼ cups buttermilk (see Note)

⅓ cup date syrup or raw honey

¼ cup dark molasses

Dash of vanilla extract

2 teaspoons baking soda

1 teaspoon fine sea salt

SPECIAL EQUIPMENT
Flour mill (optional)

If you have a flour mill, grind the oat groats, wheat berries, amaranth, lentils, barley, buckwheat, and corn to a coarse flour texture. Combine the milled grains in a large bowl with the buttermilk.

If using a blender, combine the grains, legumes, and buttermilk all at once and blend until the mixture is smooth and thick, about 3 minutes. Pour into a large bowl.

Cover the bowl and let the batter soak overnight at room temperature.

In the morning, preheat the oven to 250°F.

Combine the date syrup, molasses, and vanilla in a small bowl and add to the buttermilk mixture. Mix thoroughly with a large spoon. Add the baking soda and salt and mix well.

continued

ILONA'S CRUNCH *continued*

Line a baking sheet with parchment paper and spread out the mixture. Bake until the mixture sticks together and can be torn into pieces, approximately 1 hour.

When the crunch is cool enough to handle, break it apart with your hands into bite-sized pieces. Return the pan to the oven and bake until the pieces are dry and crunchy, another 30 minutes. Store in an airtight container for up to 1 month at room temperature or for up to 4 months in the refrigerator.

NOTE

In a couple of recipes in this chapter, I soak grains overnight in buttermilk to soften them. Real buttermilk is the liquid left over from making butter. Buttermilk is acidic and helps to break down the antinutrients in grains, making them easier to digest and improving the absorption of minerals. It also has a great effect on the final taste, adding complexity and depth. Look for real buttermilk at health food stores and farmers markets. Avoid imitation buttermilk, which is really just low-fat milk with cultures and thickening agents added to it.

HOW TO MILL YOUR OWN FLOUR

To grind your own flour, the first thing you need is a good mill. After much research, I bought the Komo Mill Duet (see Resources, page 264). It isn't cheap ($400 to $1,000, depending on specifications), but I use it almost every day—and since it's made from wood, it looks pretty sitting on my kitchen counter. I've also tried the Family Grain Mill, which costs between $150 and $550. It's easy to assemble and clean and it doesn't take up much space.

Once you own a mill, you'll discover that not only is the milling process fun, but it's also satisfying to know how healthy grinding your own grain is. You'll find it convenient and economical to buy grains in bulk, either directly from a local farm or online. I buy 40-pound bags and store them in large airtight buckets to keep out bugs and moisture. For easy access, I keep large mason jars, labeled by grain, in my pantry. When I need a particular grain, I simply pour the grain into the mill chute and grind it into fresh flour. The benefits of milling your own flour are numerous, but here are a few.

Cost: Grinding flour is more economical than buying it already ground, since grains are cheaper than flour—especially when purchased in bulk.

Flavor: The authentic flavor of home-milled flour is much more distinct than the bland taste of commercial flour.

Health: The germ has been removed from commercially ground flours. This part of the grain contains healthy, nutritious oils. It is removed to extend the shelf life of the grain/flour, which would otherwise go rancid within a day or so once the grain is milled.

Variety: Once you start buying your own grain, you'll find many different varieties, each with its own unique taste and health benefit. By grinding your own grains, and even mixing them, you can create flours that you may not find commercially.

HOME-MILLED OATMEAL

When my son, Hendrix, turned six months old and it was time for his first solid meals, I bought a grain mill. Making him freshly milled oat flour for oatmeal made me realize how much better it tasted then the store-bought oatmeal I used to eat. The oatmeal came out creamy and light, with a hint of sweetness. So I bought a flaker attachment for my mill and started making rolled oats from oat groats.

If you are not going to flake your own oatmeal, buy organic steel-cut oats from a health food store. They are the least processed oat cereal and are a healthy alternative to flaking your own. Soaking the oatmeal overnight will make it cook faster and be easier to digest.

SERVES 4

1 cup home-flaked oat groats (see page 224) or steel-cut oats

1 teaspoon lemon juice (or vinegar, yogurt, whey, or kefir)

Pinch of fine sea salt

Stewed Pears (page 98) or Slow-Cooked Applesauce (page 105), for serving

SPECIAL EQUIPMENT
Flour mill

Mix the flaked oats with 2 cups warm water and the lemon juice in a small pot. (If using steel-cut oats, add 3 cups water.) Cover and leave at room temperature overnight.

In the morning, add the salt and bring the oats to a gentle boil over medium-high heat, stirring frequently, until the oatmeal is creamy and most of the liquid has evaporated, about 5 minutes for rolled oats and 12 minutes for steel-cut oats.

Serve topped with stewed pears or applesauce.

VARIATION

Add some grated fresh apple or pear to the cooking oatmeal together with some raisins or dates to sweeten it. Serve with milk or yogurt. As an extra treat I sometimes top it with a little maple syrup, too.

OATMEAL
BAKED APPLES

Baked oatmeal has a texture similar to that of a chewy oat cookie, and stuffing this mixture into the middle of a cored apple gives it an entirely new character. The sweet flavor of the baked apple infuses the oatmeal, making it wonderfully moist. These apples are great as an after-school treat, but I always make extra to have for breakfast the next morning.

SERVES 6

1 cup home-flaked oat groats (see page 224) or old-fashioned rolled oats

2 tablespoons light brown sugar

½ cup chopped walnuts

¼ cup raisins

1½ teaspoons ground cinnamon

1 teaspoon baking powder

¼ teaspoon fine sea salt

1⅓ cups milk (ideally raw or nonhomogenized grass-fed)

½ teaspoon vanilla extract

1 large pasture-raised egg

1 tablespoon unsalted melted butter

6 large apples, such as Honeycrisp

Preheat the oven to 325°F. Line a 9-by-13-inch baking dish with parchment paper.

Combine the oats, brown sugar, walnuts, raisins, cinnamon, baking powder, and salt in a medium bowl. Mix well.

Combine the milk, vanilla, and egg in another bowl and blend well. Add the liquid mixture to the oat mixture, along with the melted butter. Mix well with a large spoon. The mixture will be very liquid.

Using a paring knife, cut off the top part of the apple with the stem and reserve the tops. Push a paring knife or an apple corer through the apple and cut around the core, leaving the bottom ½ inch of the apples intact. If necessary, use a small spoon to dig out the remaining core. Make the holes about 1 inch wide.

Place the apples on the prepared baking pan. Spoon the oatmeal mixture into the apple cavities, filling them to the top. If you have leftover oat mixture, you can bake it in a small baking dish.

Bake until the tops of the apples are golden and the oats are set, about 40 minutes. Serve warm or at room temperature. Store leftover apples covered in the refrigerator for up to 3 days.

BIRCHERMÜESLI

Birchermüesli got its name from Maximilian Bircher-Benner, a Swiss physician who was looking for a healthy breakfast for his patients more than a hundred years ago. Muesli endures as a typical Swiss breakfast food, and I've been eating it my entire life. My recipe is pretty traditional, but since it's made at home, it has a higher nutritional value than the processed muesli that comes in a box. Soaking the grains and dried fruit overnight gives a chewy consistency and improves the absorption of this nutrient-dense breakfast.

SERVES 4 (MAKES 3 CUPS)

1 cup home-flaked oat groats (see page 224) or old-fashioned rolled oats

¼ cup home-flaked rye berries (see page 224) or rye flakes

¼ cup raisins

3 tablespoons unsweetened dried blueberries

3 tablespoons dried dates, cut into pieces

¼ cup almonds, chopped

2 tablespoons raw, unsalted sunflower or pumpkin seeds

1 cup freshly squeezed orange juice

1 cup plain yogurt

Fresh fruit, crushed almonds, and extra milk or yogurt, for serving

Combine the oats, rye flakes, raisins, blueberries, dates, almonds, and seeds in a medium bowl.

Add the orange juice and yogurt. Cover and soak overnight in the refrigerator.

In the morning, stir the mixture and serve it topped with fresh fruit, crushed almonds, and extra milk or yogurt. Leftovers can be kept in the refrigerator for up to 3 days.

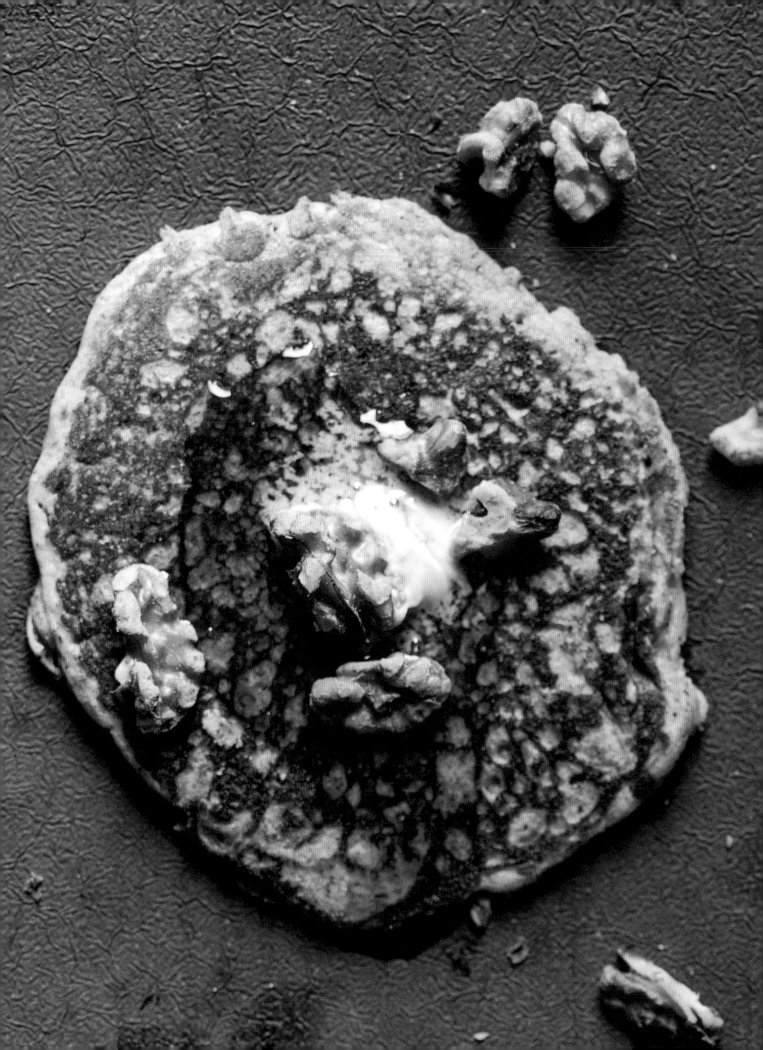

ANCIENT GRAIN PANCAKES

Using whole grains in these pancakes instead of all-purpose flour gives the nutritional value a big boost. The farro and lentils give them a robust earthy taste, while the oats lend a little sweetness. For a milder flavor, you can omit the lentils and increase the oat groats to ⅔ cup.

I usually make this recipe using my flour mill, but on a visit to my in-laws, I discovered that it can be made with an old-fashioned blender, too.

Serve these just like any other pancakes: top with butter and maple syrup or slices of fresh fruit.

SERVES 4 TO 6

1⅓ cups farro or spelt berries

⅓ cup lentils

⅓ cup oat groats

2½ cups buttermilk

2 eggs, lightly beaten

2 tablespoons maple syrup, plus more for serving

1 tablespoon butter, melted, plus more for serving

1 teaspoon baking powder

1 teaspoon fine sea salt

½ teaspoon baking soda

1 pear, diced (optional)

1 cup almonds, chopped (optional)

Coconut oil or ghee (see page 24), for frying

SPECIAL EQUIPMENT
Flour mill (optional)

If using a flour mill, grind the farro or spelt, lentils, and oats. Combine the milled grains with the buttermilk in a large bowl.

If using a blender, combine the farro or spelt, lentils, oats, and buttermilk in a blender and blend until the mixture is smooth and thick, about 3 minutes.

Cover and let the batter soak overnight at room temperature.

In the morning, combine the eggs, maple syrup, and melted butter in a small bowl. Mix into the flour mixture.

Combine the baking powder, salt, and baking soda in a separate bowl. Add to the flour mixture and mix well with a large spoon.

Fold in the pear and almonds, if using.

continued

ANCIENT GRAIN PANCAKES *continued*

Heat a large skillet or griddle on high and coat with coconut oil or ghee. Pour ⅓ cup of the batter into the pan and repeat to make as many as you can fit into the skillet or on the griddle. This batter will not be as runny as the usual pancake batter; use a spoon to spread it out a bit.

Cook until small bubbles appear on the surface, 2 to 3 minutes. Flip the pancakes and cook until golden brown, another 2 to 3 minutes. Repeat with the remaining batter. Serve the pancakes immediately or place them in the oven on a baking sheet in a single layer at 200°F.

Serve topped with butter and maple syrup. Leftovers can be kept covered in the refrigerator for up to 2 days.

CORN BREAD

Corn bread can trace its humble beginnings back to indigenous Indians, who would later introduce it to America's earliest European settlers. Nowadays it endures as an iconic part of Southern cooking. Made with freshly milled yellow dent corn, which is high in flavor and nutrition, and sweet fresh corn, this corn bread is delicious.

MAKES 1 LARGE LOAF

1¾ cups cornmeal

½ cup home-milled soft white wheat flour (see page 224) or organic whole wheat pastry flour (see Resources, page 264)

1½ cups buttermilk (ideally raw or nonhomogenized grass-fed)

½ cup milk (ideally raw or nonhomogenized grass-fed)

2 large pasture-raised eggs, beaten

1 teaspoon baking powder

1 teaspoon baking soda

1 teaspoon fine sea salt

1 tablespoon unsalted butter, at room temperature, plus more for the skillet

2 ears fresh corn, kernels removed

SPECIAL EQUIPMENT
Flour mill

Combine the cornmeal, flour, and buttermilk in a large bowl. Cover with a large plate or a dish towel and soak on the counter overnight.

Place a 10-inch cast-iron skillet in a cold oven and preheat to 420°F.

Add the milk and eggs to the soaked flour and mix well with a large spoon.

Combine the baking powder, baking soda, and salt in a small bowl and add to the flour mixture. Mix well.

Heat a small skillet over medium-high heat. Once it's hot, coat with butter and add the corn kernels. Sauté for 2 minutes. Slightly mash the corn with a potato masher or the back of a fork and add it to the flour mixture.

Remove the pan from the oven and coat it with the 1 tablespoon butter.

Pour the batter into the hot skillet and bake. After 30 minutes, check for doneness: a knife inserted into the center should come out clean and the top should be golden. Corn bread can be kept covered at room temperature for up to 1 day, in the refrigerator for up to 5 days, or in the freezer for up to 2 months.

HEARTY BREAD

Making your own bread for the first time is probably one of the most rewarding experiences ever. I love the process of baking bread. From choosing and grinding the grains to mixing it and watching it rise, every step connects you to an ancient ritual. This recipe creates a rustic loaf that has a good crust and a hearty flavor, thanks to the combination of spelt or farro flour and rye flour.

Soaking the flour overnight eliminates the need to knead the dough, rendering this a very easy recipe to make with no more than 10 minutes of active time.

MAKES 1 LARGE LOAF

2¾ cups home-milled farro flour (see page 224) or 2 cups organic spelt flour (see Resources, page 264), plus more for the work surface and ½ cup to coat the dish towel

¾ cup rye flour

1¼ teaspoons fine sea salt

½ teaspoon instant yeast

Optional additions (see Variations)

SPECIAL EQUIPMENT
Flour mill

In a large bowl, mix together the flours, salt, and yeast. Add 1½ cups plus 1 tablespoon cold water and stir together well with a large spoon. (See Note if you want to bake only half the recipe at a time.) Cover the bowl loosely with a dish towel and let the dough sit at room temperature for at least 12 hours.

After 12 hours, transfer the dough to a floured surface. If you are making any of the variations, fold those ingredients into the dough now. Stretch and fold the dough a few times. The texture will be a bit sticky, so wet your hands with some water or oil. Let the dough rest for 10 minutes, then cover it with a dish towel coated with ½ cup farro or spelt flour and let it rise at room temperature for 2 hours.

If your oven has a setting high enough to preheat a baking stone (see Resources, page 264), place the baking stone on the bottom of the oven; otherwise, place the stone on a rack set in the middle of the oven. You can use a stainless steel baking sheet if you do not have a baking stone. Preheat the oven to 500°F.

Fifteen minutes before baking the bread, lower the oven temperature to 450°F.

continued

HEARTY BREAD *continued*

Unwrap the dough, shape it into a round, and carefully transfer it to a pizza peel or flat baking sheet coated with flour. Slide it onto the baking stone in the oven.

Bake until the bread has a rich brown crust, about 40 minutes. Remove from the oven and let cool for 15 minutes before slicing. Wrap leftover bread in a large soft kitchen towel or brown paper bag and keep it at room temperature for up to 3 days (see Note).

VARIATIONS

Any of these options is great mixed into the dough.

2 tablespoons finely chopped fresh rosemary

½ cup roughly chopped pitted Kalamata olives

1 cup coarsely chopped raisins

1 cup roughly chopped pecans

1 cup coarsely chopped cranberries

1 cup roughly chopped walnuts

NOTE

This bread is so delicious right out of the oven that you and your family will probably gobble it all up. But if you won't use a full loaf within 2 days, it is best to divide the dough into two bowls after combining the flour with the yeast and water. Cover the portion you will bake with a towel and leave it on the counter for at least 12 hours. Place the other batch in the refrigerator for up to 4 days. If you are baking half a loaf, the baking time will be shorter, about 30 minutes.

SAVORY TART DOUGH

A tart crust is a good vehicle for tasting the nuances of different flours. It's a great way to see how flours can differ in texture, too. This recipe uses spelt or farro flour, which produces a firm, hearty crust. In the variations, I list other flour combinations so you can experiment. Use this tart dough with the Zucchini Tart (page 86) or Tomato Tart (page 91).

MAKES DOUGH FOR ONE 11- TO 12-INCH TART

1¾ cups home-milled farro flour (see page 224) or 1 cup organic spelt flour (see Resources, page 264), plus more for shaping the crust

1 teaspoon chopped fresh rosemary

½ teaspoon fine sea salt

¼ cup extra-virgin olive oil

2 tablespoons unsalted butter at room temperature

3 tablespoons white wine

Combine the flour, rosemary, and salt in a large bowl. Add the olive oil and butter and mix together by hand until the dough has the consistency of wet sand. Add the wine and mix together. If the dough is too dry and does not come together, add a little water.

Knead the dough by hand inside the bowl for a few minutes until it comes together as a ball. Cover with plastic and refrigerate for at least 30 minutes or overnight.

To fill and bake the tart, follow the directions for the Zucchini Tart or Tomato Tart.

VARIATIONS

If you mill your own flour, you can experiment with various grains in place of the farro. Here are some of my favorite combinations.

1⅛ cups oat flour and ¾ cup farro flour
This combination produces a flaky crust with a mellow taste.

1 cup buckwheat flour and ¾ cup soft white wheat flour
The buckwheat gives the crust a nutty taste.

½ cup farro flour, ½ cup barley flour, and ¾ cup lentil flour plus 7 tablespoons additional water
This mix makes a hearty, firm crust.

SWEET TART DOUGH

The ratio of butter to olive oil creates a delicious buttery taste and flaky texture, while the olive oil keeps it light. This tart dough is great as the base for the Peach Tart (page 113).

MAKES ONE 10-INCH TART CRUST

1 cup oat flour

1¾ cups home-milled soft white wheat flour (see page 224) or 1 cup organic whole wheat pastry flour (see Resources, page 264)

½ teaspoon fine sea salt

¼ cup extra-virgin olive oil

2 tablespoons unsalted butter, at room temperature

2 tablespoons raw honey

Combine the flours and salt in a large bowl. Add the olive oil and butter and mix together by hand until the dough has the consistency of wet sand. Add the honey and mix with a wooden spoon. If the dough is too dry and does not come together, add a little water.

Knead the dough inside the bowl for a few minutes until it comes together to form a ball. Cover with plastic and refrigerate for at least 30 minutes or overnight.

To fill and bake the tart, follow the directions for the Peach Tart.

BREAD PUDDING

Bread pudding might well be one of the most universal desserts as it usually incorporates leftover bread—something we all have on hand more often than not. There are endless variations on the recipe, and it's generally a seasonless treat, but adding vanilla and cinnamon makes it a comforting dish on a cold, wintry day. I often make this recipe with the leftover bread used to accompany a cheese fondue since the cubes are the perfect size and texture for absorbing the custard sauce.

SERVES 4

4 cups 1-inch cubes of stale bread (crusty sourdough or French bread works great)

2 cups whole milk (ideally raw or nonhomogenized grass-fed)

¼ cup raisins

¼ cup raw honey

2 large pasture-raised eggs, beaten

1 teaspoon ground cinnamon

½ teaspoon fine sea salt

¼ teaspoon grated nutmeg

1 tablespoon bourbon or rum (optional)

1½ teaspoons vanilla extract or 1 vanilla bean, split in half lengthwise

1 tablespoon butter, melted, plus more for the baking dish

1 tablespoon organic cane sugar

1 tablespoon cinnamon

In a large bowl, combine the bread cubes, milk, raisins, honey, eggs, cinnamon, salt, nutmeg, and bourbon, if using. Add the vanilla. (If using a vanilla bean, scrape the seeds into the bowl and discard the bean.) Mix. Let the bread soak for about 1 hour at room temperature.

Preheat the oven to 350°F. Coat a 9-by-13-inch baking dish with butter.

Combine the sugar and cinnamon in a small bowl.

Transfer the bread cube mixture to the prepared baking dish. Brush the top of the bread with the melted butter and sprinkle the sugar and cinnamon mixture on top.

Bake until the custard is set and a golden brown crust has formed, about 45 minutes. Let stand for 15 minutes at room temperature, then serve. Leftovers can be kept covered in the refrigerator for up to 2 days.

GIANT CHOCOLATE CHIP COOKIE

This extra-large chocolate chip cookie comes out of the oven all crisp around the edges and gooey in the center and is just sweet enough. You can serve it warm and top it with a couple of scoops of vanilla ice cream, or let it cool, break it into pieces, and serve it as individual cookies.

MAKES ONE 10-INCH COOKIE OR ABOUT 30 INDIVIDUAL COOKIES

8 tablespoons (1 stick) butter, at room temperature, plus more for greasing the pan

½ cup packed light brown sugar

2 teaspoons organic cane sugar

2 large pasture-raised eggs, lightly beaten

2 tablespoons milk (ideally raw or nonhomogenized grass-fed)

1½ teaspoons vanilla extract

2 cups home-milled soft white wheat flour (see page 224) or organic whole wheat pastry flour (see Resources, page 264)

¼ cup oat flour

1 teaspoon fine sea salt

¾ teaspoon baking soda

1½ cups chopped dark chocolate, 65% cacao or higher

1½ cups almonds or walnuts, crushed

In a large bowl, use a wooden spoon to cream the butter and sugars together just until smooth. Add the eggs, milk, and vanilla and mix until well incorporated.

Combine the flours, salt, and baking soda in another bowl and gradually stir the dry ingredients into the butter mixture. Fold in the chocolate and almonds.

Butter a 10-inch cast-iron skillet or cake pan. Spread the cookie dough mixture in the pan. Refrigerate for at least 1 hour.

Preheat the oven to 350°F.

Bake until the cookie is golden brown, about 25 minutes. Let stand for 10 minutes and serve. Leftovers can be stored in an airtight container for up to 4 days.

NOTE

You can adjust the preparation method to make individual chocolate chip cookies: Line a baking sheet with parchment paper. Form rounded tablespoon-sized balls of dough and place on the baking sheet about 3 inches apart. Refrigerate for at least 1 hour or overnight. Bake at 350°F. After 10 minutes, press the cookies flat with a spatula and bake until golden brown, about 5 minutes more. Let stand for 10 minutes before serving.

BANANA BREAD

This quick bread makes good use of those bananas that are orphaned in your fruit bowl, slowly turning dark. Overripe bananas are perfect for banana bread, so don't let them go to waste. The farro, spelt, and oat mixture adds intensity to the flavor of this banana bread, as do the buttermilk and cinnamon.

MAKES 1 LARGE LOAF

2 cups home-milled farro flour (see page 224) or 1¾ cups organic spelt flour (see Resources, page 264)

½ cup oat flour

1½ cups buttermilk (ideally raw or nonhomogenized grass-fed)

3 tablespoons butter, at room temperature, plus more for greasing the pan

3 ripe bananas

3 tablespoons raw honey

2 large pasture-raised eggs, lightly beaten

1½ teaspoons baking soda

1 teaspoon ground cinnamon

½ teaspoon fine sea salt

1½ cups chopped pecans or walnuts

Mix the flours and buttermilk in a large bowl. Cover and let soak on the counter overnight.

In the morning, preheat the oven to 350°F. Grease a 10-by-5-inch loaf pan.

Use a fork to mash the butter in a medium bowl. Mash the bananas into the butter. Add the honey and eggs and mix well.

Combine the baking soda, cinnamon, and salt in a small bowl.

Add the banana mixture to the flour mixture. Stir until just combined. Add the baking soda mixture and stir briefly. Carefully fold in the nuts.

Pour the batter into the prepared pan. Bake for 40 minutes, reduce the temperature to 325°F, and bake until golden brown, about another 30 minutes. A toothpick should come out clean when inserted into the center of the loaf. Let cool completely before slicing and serving.

WAFFLE CONES

Ice cream is the first symbolic taste of summer. Eating the cool treat on a fresh warm cone makes a most delicious dessert even more enjoyable.

You can use a waffle cone iron to produce flat disks that you then wrap around a cone. However, if you don't have a waffle cone iron, you can still make the cones by simply using a sauté pan.

MAKES ABOUT 8 CONES

¼ cup pasture-raised egg whites (from about 2 large eggs)

⅓ cup organic cane sugar

½ cup home-milled soft white wheat flour (see page 224) or organic whole wheat pastry flour (see Resources, page 264)

2 tablespoons butter, melted

2 tablespoons whole milk

½ teaspoon vanilla extract

⅛ teaspoon fine sea salt

SPECIAL EQUIPMENT
Waffle cone iron

Mix the egg whites and sugar together in a medium bowl.

Add the flour, butter, milk, vanilla, and salt, and blend well.

Spoon ¼ cup of the batter into the center of the preheated waffle cone iron and spread it out evenly using a spatula. Cook until golden brown, about 1 minute. Remove the wafer and quickly roll it around the cone-shaped mold (sold together with the waffle cone iron).

You can use a skillet instead of a waffle cone iron: Lightly grease a small skillet and heat over medium heat. Spoon ¼ cup of the batter into the center of the pan. Tilt the skillet in a circular motion so the batter covers the pan. Cook for about 3 minutes, then flip the waffle with a spatula. Cook until golden brown on both sides, about 3 minutes more, then quickly roll around a cone-shaped mold letting the sides overlap. Squeeze the tip closed so ice cream will not drip through it (if you don't have a cone mold, roll a piece of cardboard into a cone shape, tape together well, and use that).

Place the shaped cones on a rack to cool and crisp. The cones are best fresh, but they can be stored for up to 1 week in an airtight container at room temperature.

BISCOTTI

Biscotti cookies are twice baked—you first bake the dough in one piece until it is dry, then slice it into smaller cookies and bake again. This process produces a crunchy cookie that is great for dipping into coffee, tea, hot cocoa, or a dessert wine like vin santo. You can also serve biscotti with Zabaglione (page 51).

If you store biscotti in an airtight container, they will keep forever, and they make great snacks to take on camping and hiking trips.

MAKES ABOUT 20

2 cups home-milled soft white wheat flour (see page 224) or 1½ cups organic whole wheat pastry flour (see Resources, page 264)

3 large pasture-raised eggs, lightly beaten

1 cup whole almonds, coarsely chopped

½ cup organic cane sugar

2 teaspoons vanilla extract

1 teaspoon baking powder

1 teaspoon ground anise seeds

1 teaspoon orange zest

½ teaspoon ground cinnamon

⅛ teaspoon fine sea salt

Preheat the oven to 300°F. Line a baking sheet with parchment paper.

In a large bowl, combine the flour, eggs, almonds, sugar, vanilla, baking powder, anise seeds, orange zest, cinnamon, and salt and mix with a wooden spoon until the ingredients are well combined.

On the prepared baking sheet, shape the dough into a rectangle roughly 5 by 10 inches and about ¾ inch thick.

Bake until the dough is dry and firm, 25 to 30 minutes.

Cut the dough into slices about 1 by 4 inches. Bake again on one side until crunchy, about 8 minutes. Turn the cookies over and bake for another 8 minutes. Let them cool on a wire rack. As they cool, they will become even more crunchy.

RESOURCES

FOOD

The fresher your ingredients, the better your food will taste. Check localharvest.org to find farms, a CSA, or farmers markets close to you.

DATES

Dates are a great natural sweetener. Order them from Pato's Dream Date Gardens (patosdategardens.com).

FLOUR

If milling your own flour is not an option, you can try to find a local mill that sells to the public.

Great River Organic Milling (greatrivermilling.com) is a good place to purchase freshly milled flour.

Bluebird Grain Farms (bluebirdgrainfarms.com) mills to order whole-grain emmer farro, an ancient grain that adds great depth of flavor to baked goods.

GRAINS

To get the freshest grains, locate a local grain supplier. If there is no local grain supplier in your area, you can order grains online.

For farro and rye, order from Bluebird Grain Farms (bluebirdgrainfarms.com).

Other grains can be ordered at Great River Milling (greatrivermilling.com).

Store grains in airtight buckets to keep them safe from bugs and moisture. It is convenient and economical to buy in bulk the grains you use the most. For a 50-pound bag of grain, store it a 6-gallon bucket.

GROUND RAW CACAO

Raw cacao powder is available at health food stores, or you can order it online from Ultimate Superfoods (ultimatesuperfoods.com).

HERBS

If you can't find herbs locally, Mountain Rose Herbs (mountainroseherbs.com) is a great website for ordering high-quality organic herbs.

HOG CASINGS

You can try to pick up hog casings at a butcher shop, or buy them online at sausagemaker.com.

PIIMA CULTURE

Use piima culture (available at culturesforhealth.com) to make cultured butter and yogurt.

PINE NUTS

If you can't gather wild pine nuts in your area, the wild pine nuts at pinenut.com have a great flavor.

PRODUCE

When in Aspen, Jack Reed's Roots and Shoots farm stand is a must-visit. Jack is an Aspen legend who also supplies the restaurants in town. He puts together boxes of fresh fruit, vegetables, and eggs that he carefully selects from farms throughout Colorado. I also take my kids to Rock Bottom Ranch, T.R.E.E., and Sustainable Settings, where we pick fresh vegetables and gather eggs straight from the chickens.

Rock Bottom Ranch
2001 Hooks Spur Road
Basalt, CO 81621
Tel: 970-927-6760

Roots and Shoots

Sustainable Settings
6107 Colorado 133
Carbondale, CO 81623
Tel: 970-963-6107

T.R.E.E.

Aspen Tree
P.O. Box 8064
Aspen, CO 81612
Tel: 970-379-2323

RAW CACAO BUTTER

Raw cacao butter is more difficult to find at stores. You can order it online from Ultimate Superfoods (ultimatesuperfoods.com).

YOGURT STARTER

There are many varieties of yogurt starters. The tartness of yogurt is affected by the starter and creates a great range of firmness and texture in yogurt. For a creamy, mild yogurt, use yogurt starters from customprobiotics.com or culturesforhealth.com.

PARKS

To find a park close to you, visit ohranger.com, and for national parks, visit the National Park Service website (www.nps.gov).

PRESERVING MARMALADE

Check out the information at the National Center for Home Food Preservation (nchfp.uga.edu) for instructions on how to sterilize jars and prepare a canning bath.

ACKNOWLEDGMENTS

I would like to thank the following people who were instrumental in making this book:

Barbara de Vries: My heartfelt thanks to Barbara for believing in this book and helping me put it together.

Alan Hughes: Thank you for helping me with the final testing of the recipes.

Elaine Louis: Thank you for your guidance and belief that this way of life was worth sharing.

Eli and Devon Zabar: You showed us the beauty of capturing the essence of a place through our stomachs in the most simple and elegant way.

Marcel de Cock: Thank you for being a sounding board for testing ideas and honing my techniques.

Andres Fischbacher: Thank you for connecting me with local purveyors.

Aces: Thank you for showing my family and me how to live in awe of the environment and live with the land rather than on the land.

Sustainable Settings: What you guys do in Carbondale is great. Thank you for teaching me how to milk a cow and letting my children connect with the land.

T.R.E.E.: Our expeditions into the wild have brought us closer to the mountains and helped us live off the land.

Jack Reed: Your access to the best local produce has inspired many meals.

Nate King: Our mushroom hunting journey has tuned our senses to the workings of nature.

Aspen Trout Guides: Thank you for taking us to the most beautiful rivers and teaching us how to fly-fish responsibly.

I want to thank everyone at Artisan, especially Lia Ronnen and Judy Pray, for believing in me, supporting and teaching me along the way, and also giving me the creative freedom to bring this book to fruition.

INDEX

almonds:
    Almond Paste, 114
    Ancient Grains Pancakes, *236, 237, 239*
    Birchermüesli, *232, 233*
    Biscotti, *260,* 261
    blanching, 114, *115*
    Giant Chocolate Chip Cookie, *252,* 253
    Pine Nut Cookies, 153, *154*
    Trout Amandine, 144, *145*
    Wild Berry Chocolate Bars, 164–65, *165*
amaranth: Ilona's Crunch, 220, *221, 222, 223*
Ancient Grains Pancakes, *236, 237, 239*
apples, *102–3*
    Apple Cake, 202
    Apples Cooked in Hot Coals, 200, *201*
    Mulled Apple Cider, *106,* 107
    Oatmeal Baked Apples, *228,* 229
    Peach Marmalade, 108, *109*
    Slow-Cooked Applesauce, *104,* 105
    Stewed Pears, 98, *98–99*
Artichokes, Boiled, 82–83, *83*
arugula:
    Beet Salad, 76, *77*
    Chanterelle and Baby Arugula Salad, *128,* 129
Asparagus Custard Tart, *32,* 33
avocados: Kale Salad, 70, *72–73*

Banana Bread, 254, *255*
barley:
    Ilona's Crunch, 220, *221, 222, 223*
    Savory Tart Dough (var.), 247
beef:
    Twenty-Four-Hour Onion Soup, 80–81, *80*
    Vegetable Soup with Mini Meatballs, *38,* 39
beets:
    Beet Salad, 76, *77*
    Root Vegetable Chips, *64,* 65
berries:
    Birchermüesli, *232, 233*
    Fruit Rolls, 162, *163*
    Mountain Berry Marmalade, 159, *160, 161*
    Wild Berry Chocolate Bars, 164–65, *165*
    Wild Berry Fool, 156, *157*
    Zabaglione, *50,* 51
Birchermüesli, *232, 233*
Biscotti, *260,* 261
Bison Rib-Eye Steak with Porcini Mushrooms, *140,*
    141

bourbon: Bread Pudding, 250, *251*
Bratwurst, 184, *186,* 187
breads:
    Banana Bread, 254, *255*
    Bread Pudding, 250, *251*
    Corn Bread, 240, *241*
    Hearty Bread, *242,* 243–44
    Savory Tart Dough, 247
    Sweet Tart Dough, 249
bruschetta:
    Chanterelle Bruschetta, 132, *133*
    Ricotta and Roasted Fig Bruschetta, *28,* 29
Brussels sprouts: Kale Salad, 70, *72–73*
buckwheat: Savory Tart Dough (var.), 247
buttermilk, 223
    Ancient Grains Pancakes, *236, 237, 239*
    Banana Bread, 254, *255*
    Campfire Waffles, 196, 198, *199*
    Corn Bread, 240, *241*
    Ilona's Crunch, 220, *221, 222, 223*
butters:
    Cultured Butter, 22
    Garlic Scape Compound Butter, 85
    Ghee, 24
    Honey Butter, 23
    Roasted Walnut Butter, 23, *23*

cake: Apple Cake, 202
Campfire Waffles, 196, 198, *199*
carrots: Vegetable Soup with Mini Meatballs, *38,* 39
Chanterelle and Baby Arugula Salad, *128,* 129
Chanterelle Bruschetta, 132, *133*
cheese:
    Asparagus Custard Tart, *32,* 33
    Beet Salad, 76, *77*
    Chanterelle and Baby Arugula Salad, *128,* 129
    Cheese Fondue, 179–80
    Feta, Eggs, and Dandelion Greens, *126,* 127
    Kale and Feta Quiche, 34, *34*
    Porcini Fettuccine, *134,* 135
    Raclette, 183
    Ricotta, *26,* 27
    Ricotta and Roasted Fig Bruschetta, *28,* 29
    Smoked Wild Salmon Mousse, *192,* 193
    Tuscan-Grilled Pizza, 172–74, *175*
    Twenty-Four-Hour Onion Soup, 80–81, *80*
    Zucchini and Goat Cheese Quiche, *34,* 35
    Zucchini Tart, 86, *87, 88*

cherries: Clafoutis, 120, *121*
chicken:
    Country Pâté, 42, *43*, 44, 45
    Roasted Chicken, *40*, 41
chiles: Harissa, 48
chocolate:
    Chocolate Fondue, *204*, 205
    Giant Chocolate Chip Cookie, *252*, 253
    Hot Chocolate, 56, *57*
    Wild Berry Chocolate Bars, 164–65, *165*
cider: Mulled Apple Cider, *106*, 107
Clafoutis, 120, *121*
cobbler: Plum Cobbler, 117
cognac: Country Pâté, 42, *43*, 44, 45
cookies:
    Biscotti, *260*, 261
    Giant Chocolate Chip Cookie, *252*, 253
    Pine Nut Cookies, 153, *154*
corn:
    Corn Bread, 240, *241*
    Ilona's Crunch, 220, *221, 222*, 223
Country Pâté, 42, *43, 44*, 45
Cream, Whipped, 198, *199*
Cultured Butter, 22
Cured Trout, *146*, 147
custard: Asparagus Custard Tart, *32*, 33

dandelion greens: Feta, Eggs, and Dandelion
    Greens, *126*, 127
dates:
    Birchermüesli, *232*, 233
    Slow-Cooked Applesauce, *104*, 105
desserts:
    Almond Paste, 114
    Apple Cake, 202
    Apples Cooked in Hot Coals, 200, *201*
    Banana Bread, 254, *255*
    Biscotti, *260*, 261
    Bread Pudding, 250, *251*
    Chocolate Fondue, *204*, 205
    Clafoutis, 120, *121*
    Crumb Topping, 117
    Fruit Rolls, 162, *163*
    Giant Chocolate Chip Cookie, *252*, 253
    Mountain Berry Marmalade, 159, *160, 161*
    Peach Marmalade, 108, *109*
    Peach Tart, *112*, 113, *248*
    Pear Crisp, 100, *101*
    Pine Nut Cookies, 153, *154*
    Plum Cobbler, 117
    Rice Pudding, 52, *53*
    Stewed Pears, 98, *98–99*
    Sweet Tart Dough, 249

Vanilla Ice Cream, 55
Waffle Cones, *256*, 257, *258–59*
Whipped Cream, 198, *199*
Wild Berry Chocolate Bars, 164–65, *165*
Wild Berry Fool, 156, *157*
Zabaglione, *50*, 51

eggs:
    Asparagus Custard Tart, *32*, 33
    Clafoutis, 120, *121*
    Feta, Eggs, and Dandelion Greens, *126*, 127
    Kale and Feta Quiche, *34*, 34
    Mushroom Quiche, *34*, 36
    Rösti, 96–97, *97*
    Vanilla Ice Cream, 55
    Zabaglione, *50*, 51
    Zucchini and Goat Cheese Quiche, *34*, 35

farro:
    Ancient Grains Pancakes, *236*, 237, 239
    Ilona's Crunch, 220, *221, 222*, 223
    Savory Tart Dough, 247
Feta, Eggs, and Dandelion Greens, *126*, 127
figs: Ricotta and Roasted Fig Bruschetta, *28*, 29
fire for outdoor cooking, 176, *177*
fish:
    Cured Trout, *146*, 147
    Smoked Wild Salmon, 188, *189, 190–91*
    Smoked Wild Salmon Mousse, *192*, 193
    Trout Amandine, 144, *145*
    Trout Jerky, 148, *149*
flour, how to mill your own, 224
fondue:
    Cheese Fondue, 179–80
    Chocolate Fondue, *204*, 205
Fruit Rolls, 162, *163*

Garlic Scape Compound Butter, 85
Ghee, 24
Glühwein, 206, *207*
grains:
    Ancient Grains Pancakes, *236*, 237, 239
    Birchermüesli, *232*, 233
    Hearty Bread, *242*, 243–44
    how to mill your own flour, 224
    Ilona's Crunch, 220, *221, 222*, 223
    Savory Tart Dough, 247
    soaking, 218
    Sweet Tart Dough, 249
groats:
    Ancient Grains Pancakes, *236*, 237, 239
    Birchermüesli, *232*, 233
    Home-Milled Oatmeal, 226–27

groats (*cont.*)
    Ilona's Crunch, 220, *221, 222,* 223
    Oatmeal Baked Apples, *228,* 229

Harissa, 48
Hearty Bread, *242,* 243–44
Home-Milled Oatmeal, 226–27
Honey Butter, 23
Hot Chocolate, 56, *57*

ice cream:
    Vanilla Ice Cream, 55
    Waffle Cones, *256,* 257, *258–59*
Ilona's Crunch, 220, *221, 222,* 223

Kale and Feta Quiche, 34, *34*
Kale Salad, 70, *72–73*

Lamb Sausage, 46, 47–48
lentils:
    Ilona's Crunch, 220, *221, 222,* 223
    Savory Tart Dough (var.), 247
liver: Country Pâté, 42, *43, 44,* 45

marmalade:
    Mountain Berry Marmalade, 159, *160, 161*
    Peach Marmalade, 108, *109*
milk:
    Bread Pudding, 250, *251*
    Clafoutis, 120, *121*
    Corn Bread, 240, *241*
    grass-fed, 20
    Homemade Yogurt, *18,* 19
    Hot Chocolate, 56, *57*
    Oatmeal Baked Apples, *228,* 229
    Rice Pudding, 52, *53*
    Ricotta, *26,* 27
Mountain Berry Marmalade, 159, *160, 161*
Mulled Apple Cider, *106,* 107
mushrooms:
    Bison Rib-Eye Steak with Porcini Mushrooms, *140,* 141
    Chanterelle and Baby Arugula Salad, *128,* 129
    Chanterelle Bruschetta, 132, *133*
    Home-Dried Porcini Mushrooms, 136, *137*
    Mushroom Quiche, *34,* 36
    Porcini Fettuccine, *134,* 135
    Tuscan-Grilled Pizza, 172–74, *175*

oats:
    Birchermüesli, *232,* 233
    Home-Milled Oatmeal, 226–27
    Ilona's Crunch, 220, *221, 222,* 223

Oatmeal Baked Apples, *228,* 229
Pear Crisp, 100, *101*
Savory Tart Dough (var.), 247
onions: Twenty-Four-Hour Onion Soup, 80–81, *80*

pancakes: Ancient Grains Pancakes, *236,* 237, 239
pasta: Porcini Fettuccine, *134,* 135
pastry:
    Savory Tart Dough, 247
    Sweet Tart Dough, 249
pâté: Country Pâté, 42, *43, 44,* 45
peaches:
    Peach Marmalade, 108, *109*
    Peach Tart, *112,* 113, *248*
pears:
    Ancient Grains Pancakes, *236, 237,* 239
    Pear Crisp, 100, *101*
    Stewed Pears, 98, *98–99*
pecans: Banana Bread, 254, *255*
peppers: Harissa, 48
Pheasant Confit, 150, *151*
piima culture, 22
Pine Needle Tea, 210, *211*
Pine Nut Cookies, 153, *154*
pizza: Tuscan-Grilled Pizza, 172–74, *175*
Plum Cobbler, 117
popcorn: Rosemary-Flavored Popcorn, 194, *195*
Porcini Fettuccine, *134,* 135
pork:
    Bratwurst, 184, *186,* 187
    Country Pâté, 42, *43, 44,* 45
    Lamb Sausage, 46, 47–48
potatoes:
    Baked Potato Chips, 68, *69*
    Crispy Roasted Potatoes, *94,* 95
    Raclette, 183
    Rösti, 96–97, *97*
    Vegetable Soup with Mini Meatballs, *38,* 39
puddings:
    Bread Pudding, 250, *251*
    Rice Pudding, 52, *53*

quiche:
    Kale and Feta Quiche, 34, *34*
    Mushroom Quiche, *34,* 36
    Zucchini and Goat Cheese Quiche, *34,* 35

Raclette, 183
raisins:
    Apples Cooked in Hot Coals, 200, *201*
    Birchermüesli, *232,* 233
    Bread Pudding, 250, *251*

Oatmeal Baked Apples, *228*, 229
Rice Pudding, 52, *53*
Red Clover Iced Tea, 166
Rice Pudding, 52, *53*
Ricotta, *26*, 27
Ricotta and Roasted Fig Bruschetta, *28*, 29
Root Vegetable Chips, *64*, 65
Rosemary-Flavored Popcorn, 194, *195*
Rösti, 96–97, *97*
rum: Bread Pudding, 250, *251*

salads:
  Beet Salad, 76, *77*
  Chanterelle and Baby Arugula Salad, *128*, 129
  Kale Salad, 70, *72–73*
salmon:
  Smoked Wild Salmon, 188, *189*, *190–91*
  Smoked Wild Salmon Mousse, *192*, 193
sausage:
  Bratwurst, 184, *186*, 187
  Lamb Sausage, 46, *47–48*
Savory Tart Dough, 247
Smoked Wild Salmon, 188, *189*, *190–91*
Smoked Wild Salmon Mousse, *192*, 193
soups:
  Twenty-Four-Hour Onion Soup, 80–81, *80*
  Vegetable Soup with Mini Meatballs, *38*, 39
spelt:
  Ancient Grains Pancakes, *236*, 237, 239
  Ilona's Crunch, 220, *221*, *222*, 223
  Savory Tart Dough, 247
steak: **Bison Rib-Eye Steak with Porcini**
      Mushrooms, *140*, 141
Sun-Dried Tomatoes, 92, *93*
sweet potatoes, Root Vegetable Chips, *64*, 65
Sweet Tart Dough, 249

tarts:
  Asparagus Custard Tart, *32*, 33
  Peach Tart, *112*, 113, *248*
  Savory Tart Dough, 247
  Sweet Tart Dough, 249
  Tomato Tart, 88, *90*, 91
  Zucchini Tart, 86, *87*, 88
tea:
  Pine Needle Tea, 210, *211*
  Red Clover Iced Tea, 166

tomatoes:
  Sun-Dried Tomatoes, 92, *93*
  Tomato Tart, 88, *90*, 91
  Tuscan-Grilled Pizza, 172–74, *175*
  Vegetable Soup with Mini Meatballs, *38*,
    39
Trout, Cured, *146*, 147
Trout Amandine, 144, *145*
Trout Jerky, 148, *149*
Tuscan-Grilled Pizza, 172–74, *175*
Twenty-Four-Hour Onion Soup, 80–81, *80*

Vanilla Ice Cream, 55
veal: Bratwurst, 184, *186*, 187
vegetables:
  Root Vegetable Chips, *64*, 65
  Vegetable Soup with Mini Meatballs, *38*,
    39
Vinaigrette, 82

Waffle Cones, *256*, 257, *258–59*
waffles: Campfire Waffles, 196, 198, *199*
walnuts:
  Apple Cake, 202
  Apples Cooked in Hot Coals, 200, *201*
  Banana Bread, 254, *255*
  Giant Chocolate Chip Cookie, *252*, 253
  Oatmeal Baked Apples, *228*, 229
  Pear Crisp, 100, *101*
  Roasted Walnut Butter, 23, *23*
wheat berries: Ilona's Crunch, 220, *221*, *222*,
  223
Whipped Cream, 198, *199*
wine:
  Cheese Fondue, 179–80
  Glühwein, 206, *207*
  Porcini Fettuccine, *134*, 135
  Twenty-Four-Hour Onion Soup, 80–81, *80*
  Zabaglione, *50*, 51

yogurt:
  Birchermüesli, *232*, 233
  Homemade Yogurt, *18*, 19

Zabaglione, *50*, 51
Zucchini and Goat Cheese Quiche, *34*, 35
Zucchini Tart, 86, *87*, *88*

CONVERSIONS

WEIGHTS			VOLUME			OVEN TEMPERATURE			
US/UK	METRIC		AMERICAN	IMPERIAL	METRIC		°F	°C	GAS MARK
¼ oz	7 g		¼ tsp		1.25 ml	VERY COOL	250–275	130–140	½–1
½ oz	15 g		½ tsp		2.5 ml	COOL	300	148	2
1 oz	30 g		1 tsp		5 ml	WARM	325	163	3
2 oz	55 g		½ tbsp (1½ tsp)		7.5 ml	MEDIUM	350	177	4
3 oz	85 g		1 tbsp (3 tsp)		15 ml	MEDIUM HOT	375–400	190–204	5–6
4 oz	115 g		¼ cup (4 tbsp)	2 fl oz	60 ml	HOT	425	218	7
5 oz	140 g		⅓ cup (5 tbsp)	2½ fl oz	75 ml	VERY HOT	450–475	232–245	8–9
6 oz	170 g		½ cup (8 tbsp)	4 fl oz	125 ml				
7 oz	200 g		⅔ cup (10 tbsp)	5 fl oz	150 ml				
8 oz (½ lb)	225 g		¾ cup (12 tbsp)	6 fl oz	175 ml				
9 oz	255 g		1 cup (16 tbsp)	8 fl oz	250 ml				
10 oz	285 g		1¼ cups	10 fl oz	300 ml				
11 oz	310 g		1½ cups	12 fl oz	350 ml				
12 oz	340 g		1 pint (2 cups)	16 fl oz	500 ml				
13 oz	370 g		2½ cups	20 fl oz (1 pint)	625 ml				
14 oz	400 g		5 cups	40 fl oz (1 qt)	1.25 l				
15 oz	425 g								
16 oz (1 lb)	450 g								